WILD GOOSE COUNTRY

WILD GOOSE COUNTRY

Horicon Marsh to Horseshoe Island

by Robert E. Gard

photography by Edgar G. Mueller

WISCONSIN HOUSE BOOK PUBLISHERS

BOOKS BY ROBERT E. GARD

A Woman of No Importance
Wisconsin Sketches
The Trail of the Serpent
Wild Goose Marsh
Down In the Valleys
This Is Wisconsin
University Madison USA
Wisconsin Lore
The Romance of Wisconsin Place Names
The Puzzle of Roanoke
The Cardiff Giant
Devil Red
Act 9
The Error of Sexton Jones
Wisconsin Is My Doorstep
Grassroots Theater

First Edition
ISBN 0-88361-039-6
Library of Congress Card Number 75-18194

Copyrighted 1975 by Robert E. Gard and Edgar G. Mueller. All rights reserved.
Design and Line Drawings by Susan Charlebois.

Printed in the United States of American for Wisconsin House Book Publishers
by Straus Printing and Publishing Co., Inc., Madison, Wisconsin

The author's dedication is made with grateful appreciation to Walter Scott, always a friend of wildlife, who has been so influential in creating a better relationship between man and bird.

The photographer's dedication is made to the many kind and thoughtful friends who throughout the years have helped by suggesting original photographic situations and subjects.

ACKNOWLEDGMENTS

When I began to try to create a character who cared so much about the wetlands that his whole life revolved around them, I found that I was probably thinking about a number of individuals who loved the marsh and lived it every day. Many of these great personalities I did not have the fortune to know personally because they were gone before I entered the scene, but the lore about them was prevalent. Joe Malone represents all of them; he is really the essence of men like Bill Field, Bill Roebe, George Hall, Barnie Wanie, Franklin Burrow, Lee Burrow, Willard Firehammer, John Strook, Leo Gehrke, Frank Bossman, Adam Port, Curley Radke, Ed Lechner, Dr. John Karsten, Lester Mieske, George Spettel, Bill Missling and Judge Clarence Traeger.

There were others, too, and a lot of them who worked, fished, hunted and trapped on the marsh and who had a hand in the return of the Canada Geese. I heard stories told by some of the individuals listed, and others by people not listed. Lives were and are filled with dreams about the old days and time continues to be marked by the arrival of the flock, the way the muskrats thrive and how good the fishing is.

I certainly need to acknowledge the unselfish help given to me by the Wildlife Ecology Department of the University of Wisconsin; by a most helpful graduate student in that department, Scott Craven; by Frank King, Ruth Hine and Walter Scott of the Department of Natural Resources of Wisconsin.

I need to remember some friends who helped me: L. G. Sorden and Jim Batt, also. Dr. Harold Rusch who boated me through the Marsh several times.

Lastly, I want to mention my friend and Wisconsin-born author, Sigrud Olsen who inspired some of the thoughts expressed in this book.

In the early morning before dawn, I hear the sound of wings.

I see them coming in the early light, their bodies dark against the breaking day.

It seems as though the air is theirs alone.

Their story is like mine; we are wanderers in spirit; they transport me to wonder.

There were four goslings in the family that had hatched on the tiny island in the pothole. The pothole was about fifty miles up the west side of James Bay, inland from the mouth of the Albany River in Ontario Province. In that country the potholes were numerous and very close together, so that the ponds were separated by very narrow strips of land, sometimes quite thickly, and sometimes not at all.

There had been no real difficulty during their infanthood. They all survived the hazards: the storms, the foxes, and the Indians who knew where to search for geese in that region. Onetime, three goslings from a brood in a neighboring pond tried to join their family. The gander, their father, drove them away fiercely, and their mother joined him. Their father led them afield from the nesting island, searching for food, and sometimes they found berries and green things, and the little ones found some insects which they gobbled eagerly. Nothing happened to any of the family, and the little geese grew and became stronger. They developed baby feathers, then the stronger feathers, and little by little, they gained strength and water skills until by August they could fly. The gander led them in many flights, then, as though in preparation for the long, long flight they would soon have to make.

The goslings stayed very close to their mother and father, and even as the babes grew, the parents did not diminish their concern and interest. During the migration flight, with the gander leading and the family in shifting patterns behind and alongside him, the parents kept a watch on their brood, and the family communicated with one another by short, sharp honks that told each one something of value; where they were, perhaps, or the direction of the wind, or whether they were to fly higher or lower. Nobody knows what the wild goose says, but everyone knows that they do speak to one another, and that directions are given.

This particular goose family, along with thousands of other Canada geese, flew their usual route — one that some of them had flown dozens of times, and one that many had never flown at all. But the young ones noted the landmarks, the great lake, the cities, the patterns of agricultural lands. But there was no stopping until the leaders sighted the first of their great stopovers. They began to circle when they came into the vicinity of the great Horicon Marsh in Wisconsin. To them there was no state, no county, no city limit. They were conscious only of the marsh as their domain, and that there was where corn stood waiting in the fields.

The great circling movements grew smaller and lower, and at last the leading birds peeled away from the flock and circled lower and lower, the rest following, until the birds landed on one of the wide open areas where the Rock River spreads into the marsh through an old, old riverbed. Here the large flock settled, for it was near evening time. And here they would spend the night, resting, talking softly among the family groups, thinking perhaps of the lush feeding they would begin on the morrow, among the standing cornstalks.

All during late October and into November, the family fed. Each day the gander led them up and out of the marsh, flying by routes he knew well, across to the fields;

and when the corn at the marsh was exhausted, he led them out of the sanctuary, across the edges of the marsh and private farmlands to outlying fields in which the geese had no legal right, but where there was a great deal of corn to glean. Sometimes he led them into fields where the corn was yet unharvested, and here they sometimes had difficulty with angry farmers who came, making loud noises and waving large cloths. There were also, in some of these fields, strange devices that exploded with a noise much, much greater than a hunter's gun. And these devices gave out their great noises regularly, very frightening at first to the younger geese who had never seen or heard the things before, but not frightening at all to the gander and his mate. For they knew that the cannons were placed to drive them from the fields, and that they expelled no shot or ball. They knew that the great sounds would not hurt them, and often they fed within a rod or two of the cannon. Soon the younger ones imitated their parents.

The hunters were a problem to the family. At the edges of the marsh the geese, flying very high — for the gander was a wise, wise bird — could see the waiting men. There were hunters crouching in the blinds; and the old gander knew what a blind was. He could tell where the pits were dug, or what the standing shocks of corn meant in the middle of already harvested fields. He was careful that his family stay clear of the hunters. But some families did not learn, and did not heed; and many of the younger geese fell from the air, mortally hurt or killed outright with a single blast of a hunter's gun.

Once the family, flying high above, saw an entire family of geese killed in an instant. There had been eight in that family group; and the goslings had hatched in a pond near theirs. One after another the family plunged to earth; and the old gander perhaps communicated to his young ones the dangers of flying too low over certain sections, too carelessly with only hunger in mind. For it was hunger that led the geese so much into danger. Some, when hungry, would heed nothing, but went directly by the shortest possible way to the feeding ground.

The young geese watched their father, and they did learn, but they were, after all, not yet eight months old, and they had so many things to learn.

It would be two, perhaps even three years before the goslings would take mates of their own. If they could remain and learn from their father for that full time, then they, too, would become wise.

Sometimes, on a Sunday at the Horicon Marsh, and other days as well, the family would gather with thousands of others on a broad rye field near the highway at the northern end of the marsh. There the birds rested in the sun, talking, so that their voices became a continuous and everchanging wall of sound. The people, hundreds and hundreds, lined the highway, their cars pulled out onto the shoulders, and watched the geese. Many had binoculars; many others just watched in silent amazement at the numbers of the geese, noting their actions, picking out this one or that one which seemed particularly large. There were some snow geese and blue geese among the Canadas, and the people watched the entire, wonderful panorama; they marveled at the show. Many of the people returned year after year to the marsh to see the fall's wild goose pageant.

Of the amazement of human beings the geese knew and cared nothing. They merely followed their bent, doing those things that were pleasant and necessary to do. If there was no food at the marsh they would leave. The people mattered not at all, though the birds had become accustomed to the humans and paid small attention. The geese knew that they were safe in the field, and that there were no guns among the crowds on the highway.

Yet danger and death were realities. One day one of the young geese of the family became confused and departed from the family group. It was while they were flying east, over the marsh's edge, and the young one, not hearing the calls, came quite low, flying alone, and from above, frantically, the family saw their brother killed. The charge took him directly. His feathers flew. And he collapsed in air, crumbling and withering, it seemed, and plunged to the earth into the cornfield not very far from the man whose blast had brought him down.

So there were three of the young left, and they seemed to draw closer to their parents. The little family grew restive in November, as so many others were restless when the wind increased and the temperature dropped. The first hard freezes left the ice quite thick on the ditches. There was still open water, but the flock knew that it was time for them to move on.

Actually, it was the gander, the father, who was one of the first to go. He led his brood up and up, as though to take them to the feeding grounds, but he did not. He went higher and higher, circling, up and up, and then, without warning, except to utter sharp, short commands, he led them south.

They passed high over Madison, over the University of Wisconsin. They passed over Lake Koshkonong, striking south along the Rock River, and following the Rock until it joined the Mississippi. There was a wind from the rear and the birds flew very fast, sometimes sixty miles an hour. They struck the Mississippi and followed the great river, south and south, seeing many other geese and ducks, and they came at last to the Horseshoe Lake refuge. Here they knew there would be new stands of corn, and that the birds who arrived at the fields first would reap a marvelous harvest. As they came in they could see the cypress trees; trunks in the water, and the head quarters, buildings with pens where geese were trapped and banded. The gander and his mate had never been banded.

The old gander did not take them directly to the corn. He flew instead to the sandbar which he knew so well, and had rested on so many, many times. It was a great bar that went quite far out into the stream of the Mississippi, and at times it was under water, but this time it was not. Here the family lighted, and here they renewed the sand in their crops, so that when they ate the corn it would be digested.

The flock stayed on the bar all night. In the early morning there was gunfire to the south of them, and the gander led them up and away from the river.

During the time in Illinois, the family escaped the hunters and returned safely to the north in the spring. They stopped again at Horicon, resting and eating, and when the chemistry that was within them told them it was time to head north, the gander led them up and away. They arrived in the area of the Albany River before the snow had melted — well before, for it was a late season — and before the ice had gone. They waited with patience, feeding where they could, and the gander knew where to take them so that the Indian hunters would not find them. Many of the other geese fell to the Indian guns. When the ice had gone and the sun warmed and the snow melted, the goose began to build her nest. She built it in the same spot that the goslings had been hatched, and the gander stood guard with his last year's young; but when the goose had made her nest and the egg laying began, the young geese were terrified and bewildered by the behavior of their parents. Instead of the calm watchfulness which their parents had always maintained, and the security the young birds felt, a completely different thing was taking place. The old birds became suddenly heartless, cruel, and uncaring. They drove the young ones away from the nesting place, and when they returned, crying pitifully, they were chased away again. Many times it happened, the gander administered hard blows with wings and bill, and the goose came to help, uttering sharp cries and viciously attacking those whom a day before she had caressed. And finally, the three young ones were defeated. They went slowly and sadly away, not understanding the treatment, but understanding that they were not wanted.

They went far, joining a group of other displaced young ones and a few mateless adults. Together they foraged, and slowly they forgot their parents.

In August, more than a year after they were born, the young geese were more mature, but still not fully developed, and far less in wisdom than older, more experienced geese. At Horicon one of the three, a female, was shot down; and when the other two came back frantically searching for her, one of them was shot. The other circled high, forlorn, and finally joined other birds. The last gosling was a strong young gander. He had learned something from seeing his sister and brother killed, and he remembered the lessons his father had tried to teach. He flew very high out of the refuge, and his eyes, wary now and very keen, could discern the hidden blinds and the men waiting. Often he caught the glint of gunmetal, or he saw the flesh of an arm, or the reflection of sun off a bottle. He kept away from the hunters and he survived.

In Illinois, at the Crab Orchard refuge where he went with a mateless flight, he found a great deal of company. He was over a year old now, and heavier than most. He was too young still to mate. Next season he would find a mate, but now he must wait impatiently, watching the love games of others, feeling the male angers rise. He fought an old gander and nearly did him great damage, seizing again and again the feathers at the back of the neck, striving, wanting to kill. The other gander fled, and the young gander, son of a wise father, stood alone on his small section of graze. He did not know that the old gander he had fought was his father; and the father did not recognize his son.

The old gander, mateless for a year now, for his mate, inseparable for four seasons, had recently been killed, wandered among the other mateless birds. He now seldom made threatening moves, and his head and feather displays were halfhearted. One of the workmen at the Horicon refuge, a man named Joe Malone, had identified the gander for three years and had watched for his return because the bird seemed so proud, so arrogant, so overbearing toward other ganders, and so willing to make belligerent moves.

The gander paid no real attention to the men, though, and though he eyed them with suspicion, gave the impression that he could hardly care less what happened to him. Joe thought the heart had been taken out of the gander and felt very sorry for him. There was still a certain air about the gander that made him recognizable, and Joe thought that certainly he must have been one of the proud ones, a singular creature, and now, somehow, he was nothing.

Once Joe saw the gander at the edge of a flock and saw how a younger gander made him retreat. It was as though the old gander didn't care. In Joe's imagination, which had increased as he grew older, he could believe that the gander was brokenhearted, and that he was deathbound. In his fantasy, Joe made up a whole set of experiences which he believed the goose might remember; the time when the gander was two years old, strong, a little larger than the other geese perhaps, and definitely more defiant. He figured that the goose could certainly remember how he had selected his mate, a goose the same age as himself, and how he had defended his right to her among all others, neck stretched out, bill agape, hissing angrily, the feathers rising on his neck, and this was usually enough to frighten off a rival. If not, then the rush, the push and attack, the body contact, and the angry bill seizing feathers on neck or head. Once or twice he beat other ganders with his wings. But he became known as being fierce and angry and the other birds let him alone. When he had established his territory and defended it successfully, he honked loudly in triumph and flapped his wings, and his mate joined him in these expressions of gratification.

And there was the ritual of mating. It was a water game which the gander would not forget. It happened at the wintering grounds in late February, and there was no explanation for the suddenness of the erotic behavior of the flock. The unmated ones often competed with one another, and the young males played with each other, one the male, one the female, wrestling in the water. And the mated ones began the endless cycles of the ritual love.

The gander's mate started it, really, swimming slowly away from him, ducking her head deeply into the water and submerging her body, the breast and shoulders, until only the rear part of her thrust upward. The gander, swimming close beside her instantly upended, copying her movement, and they both drew their heads out of the water at about the same instant, and swam a little apart to repeat the movement again and again. It was almost like a start, a beginning, of a strange dance that could have but one climax, ages old, repeated season after season for half a million years, perhaps; expressing the stimulus of instinct, of prepared tissue, of sun, moon, of the dark spirit of wild magic. And again the female turned in the water to face her mate and dipped her head again and again into the water, bringing it out rapidly and splashing water up and over, while her mate facing her does the same thing, and together, repeating and repeating, the two lovers perform the rite, the dance of love, or the repeated movements of the prelove dance. Perhaps the strange dipping and throwing of the water recalled to them the ritual of feeding; the delving into shallow water, the exploration of the bottom of marsh waters for roots and seeds. The rituals of one phase of life do determine others. Geese are no different from men in that the repetitions of celebrations appear again and again in strange ways, but are interlinked.

The dipping dance occurs many times, and when it has reached its climax, the gander has come alongside and a little back of his mate. The female then flattens herself in the water, stretches out her neck while the gander seizes her by the feathers on her back. As the gander mounts on top of her, he grasps the feathers on her neck. The weight of the gander pushes the mate down and down. She is at times almost completely submerged, while the union, which lasts only a few seconds, takes place.

Then after it is over, other rituals begin. The gander, coming off his mate, faces her with feathers ruffled on his neck and head held high. His bill points upwards; he utters a low, throaty cry, he rises in the water, triumphant, flapping wings, crying, and both gander and mate wash themselves, flinging water, preening, rubbing bill and heads across their backs. Together the birds leave the water, come onto the shore, and standing near each other, they dress and preen their feathers for a long while.

The ritual of love takes place always in the water, and the water, traditional sauce of life, is a fitting place for the mating of the wild geese.

Mates are not often interfered with during the lovemaking, but sometimes they are observed; others of the flock may surround them and join them in celebration of the successful termination of the rite. Their cries join those of the gander, and their wings beat in joyful recognition of the act of life. The ritual precedes the migration of spring, and within the act is the symphony of the cycles; the seasons, the flights, the feeding, the nesting, the bitter fights, and the coming to rest upon familiar water and earth.

Their power is in me and their direction is the direction of my spirit.

The sound pounds, beats and lifts.

8

My friend, Sigrud Olsen, says that you have to have a feeling for wilderness in your life, the wild, or you don't know your soul.

Moving very carefully so that he did not disturb Mary, Joe Malone arose from the bed where he had slept with her for more than forty-five years. Joe moved a little stiffly, listening to her low breathing, and wondered for an instant whether she would feel more like going outside tomorrow. He placed a hand on the bed; he felt the smooth maple wood, and in the dark he pictured the whole bed, the carved footboard, and the higher carved headboard, with Mary's pillows against it. It was a bed they had inherited from Mary's mother. A lot of my life has been in this bed, Joe thought, and smiled to remember how he really didn't enjoy sleeping anyplace else.

Joe went slowly to the window through the darkened room. He knew the placement of every piece of furniture: the dresser, oak, at the side, with the two small lamps on it, and the mirror that had belonged to his Aunt Sarah. Near the bed, positioned so that he could sit there and watch television in the evenings, was the Boston rocker that had been his grandmother's, and at the side of the room were the two straight chairs that Aunt Sarah had used when she was nursing Grandfather Malone during his last illness.

Joe touched the pieces as he passed them — he could go about the room with his eyes closed, and did, sometimes, when he was restless and arose in the night. He drifted to the window and pulled aside the drape that Mary had sewn from material her sister had given her — heavy, silken, and a bit strange, Joe considered, because he was always a simple-living man, and Mary was the same way, really, though she had more of a taste for richer, silken things and china, than he did.

His fingers pulled aside the drape, and he looked out into the night.

The moon had finally risen, Joe saw, and he never failed, when he got up at night at this time of year, to wait breathlessly on the nights of the moon for the sight that might happen. Many times he had seen the wild geese cross the moon, and the sight was always new, and so beautiful that he lived eternity in an instant. For the most part, the birds rested during the night, using the backwaters and the marsh ponds in the refuge; but in the migration season they often flew in from the north, or if winds had delayed them, they might be late getting back to the refuge from the far-out feeding grounds. Then they might cross the moon, and to Joe this sight was always full of marvel.

Mary raised on an elbow and said sleepily, "Joe? Joe, can't you come back to bed?"

"I'm restless," he said, as he always did when she questioned him; and he knew that his answer satisfied her, for it had come to mean, over the years, so many, many things.

It meant his deep and constant concern for the birds; for their arrival in the fall and spring, and the preparation that had been made for them. It meant his love of the marsh itself, for the wide reaches of the tall grass and cattail swamps, for the bayous, the ditches, the widening out of the river as it meandered south through the marshlands. It meant his memories of early day wanderings at marsh edges, or in the ditches in his canoe to watch the birds and to hear their calls. Sometimes, too, Mary had gone with him, especially after the children were grown, for they both loved the wetlands, and their home had been chosen long, long ago in a location within the marsh itself where they could live among the wildlife.

Their home, he knew, had also been so important to their son and daughter, Steve and Betty; both of them had developed their love of the wildlife right here at home, in the front yard, and both of them had carried their concern for the wild ones right on into college. Both were now making their living at conservation work, and both were doing what they most wanted to do. Lucky.

"Come on back to bed," Mary said.

"Nope. I'm going outside."

"Well, all right."

He stood a while longer at the window and heard the wind around the housetop and in the cottonwood tree that shaded the front yard. He thought he could hear the sleepy calling of the resting Canadas far off, but he couldn't be quite sure. The migration started to come in yesterday; and with the colder weather now in the far north, the birds would be coming in great flights by day and by night. It was a strange thing with Joe, at this time of year he himself suffered actual changes; the deep sense of restlessness grew more and more acute, as though he, too, must ready himself for the long flight. He grew impatient, even snappish with Mary, and he regretted it, though he knew that she understood. He felt the call, he supposed, and had never been rightly able to understand his sensations. He only knew that he seemed to grow leaner, more alert, acute to sounds and feelings; more sensitive to the changing colors and sights of the marsh — to the rattle of the drying grasses and pods, to the fall flowers and the rustle of leaves. He wondered whether he would feel the sensations for the remainder of his life. He supposed he would. Patterns of life and work, even when one was no longer doing active work in a daily job, didn't change all that much. He'd learned to rest somewhat more than he used to. People told him that was good, but he felt quite well and didn't understand, really, why they had made him stop his job four years ago when he was actually in the real prime of his life.

"I didn't want to stop," he said aloud.

"What did you say, Joe?"

"Oh, nothing. I was just talking to myself."

"Will you be out long?"

"I don't know. Probably not."

"You're not going to fish!"

"I don't know. I might."

"Well, be careful."

"Oh, I will."

He went, without turning on the light, to the Boston rocker where his pants were draped over the top. Mary always urged that he put his garments on a hanger in the closet, but he always wanted his trousers near at hand. Especially in his working days it had sometimes been necessary to get dressed in a hurry; in the nights when there were fires on the marsh, he'd always been there as soon as he could, helping any way he could, though when the fires had gotten started there wasn't too much anybody could do.

There hadn't been a fire for a long while, not since they had restored the water to the marsh, after the dam had been rebuilt at Horicon. Anyway, his pants were there across the chair back, and he carefully got his legs into them, pulled them over his cotton long-legged underwear, and fastened the waist.

The zipper made a tiny sound, and Mary said, almost inaudibly, "Don't stay out all night, Joe.

"I won't."

He went out, in the dark still, to the small kitchen, and glanced at the wall clock, the oak one with a gingerbread frieze that his mother had owned all of her married life. The time was half-past two. He put the kettle on to boil, and took his woolen shirt and jacket from the kitchen doorway closet. While he waited for the water, he put on the garments and laced up the heavy shoes. When the water was ready he made tea, stirred in sugar, and carried the cup out onto the back porch.

He wondered how many mornings he had stood on the porch, very early, listening, searching the night sky, hoping for rare sights and muted far sounds.

Joe finished the tea, stepped inside, set the cup back on the kitchen table that Mary kept covered with the red and white checked cloth — the same kind of cloth she had used for more than forty years. He went back to the porch and lifted the metal rod and spinning reel off the hooks. He kept bait in cardboard milk containers in the bottom of the old refrigerator in the porch corner, and he took out a carton of night crawlers. The air had a bit of a nip, he thought, and he finally took his heavy jacket off the nail on the porch wall. His crumpled felt hat on, he walked slowly down the steps and into the backyard.

The night sky was lighted by the far, low moon. There was wind in the dooryard trees. He stood a moment considering whether to take the boat, or to walk down the side of the marsh ditch to the fishing hole near the large oak. He decided on the boat.

The boat was flatbottom and wooden, very old, but in superior shape. He kept it that way, and he was sure that he would never have any other boat for the ditch fishing. He wouldn't use a motor — he had used one when he worked for the state; you had to then, to save time, but now, and in anything he did privately on the river or in the marsh, he would tolerate no motor. He loved the silence, the small sounds of oars and the gentle dip of water. He loved the slow, easy movements, and the responsive urges of the boat in still water. Most of all, he cherished the bird sounds he could hear and identify in the stillness. Now a loon was calling, far-off in the marsh. He pushed the boat away from the dock and let it drift a moment.

Overhead, as the boat drifted away from the shore, the moon emerged among trees, and as he watched there was movement in the sky. Low sounds, a rip, dim beatings, wings, and as he stared upward, the flight of the Canadas came across the moon. The sight was a holy one to him; he realized that he was witnessing a private, yet common reality, his religion, his knowledge of life supreme, of creatures in the sky and across the moon.

Low sounds of their voices, the wild, the nonunderstandable. All of his life he had waited for such moments. And when he died his wish was that he could possess a sense of the wild, of far beauty, of swiftly moving bodies.

Perhaps fall was his favorite time on the marsh, for it was then that the goose flock enriched both sky and land, and the cornfields were filled with reaching, restless necks and searching bills.

He drifted further and sat watching, listening, never baiting his hook until the early light of morning began to filter through the tall trees on the eastern edge of the Horicon Marsh.

Whenever Joe Malone got to remembering how things had been, and tried to put into perspective the way the reality of the marsh had been achieved as a wildlife refuge, he thought always about Charles Gray. It had begun when Joe was twenty-one, a farm boy living on the far western edge of the Horicon Marsh. The time was the 1920s. Joe finished high school and farmed with his father for a couple of years until it was apparent that there was no future for both of them on the home place. In the summers, along with helping at home, he worked with the haymen who cut the heavy marsh meadow grass, baled it, and hauled the bales into Milwaukee to the breweries. They used the hay to wrap beer bottles in those days. And in the winter Joe trapped muskrats, but it wasn't very profitable because it was coming into the depression years, and the skins brought little at the fur markets. The start of his real job occurred when the official from the state Conservation Department at Madison came to the marsh on an inspection trip. He brought with him three members of the state legislature, because the state was then considering buying land for a wildlife refuge. Their Chrysler stuck deep in the mud alongside the Malone cornfield, clear up to the hubcaps, and Joe, using his father's heavy team of Belgians, had managed to snake them out. He would take no pay, and they joked together. The whole occasion had been pleasant, and Joe's German mother asked the men in for coffee and homemade bread.

Later on, the Madison official came back several times, always stopping at the Malone farm to talk, and he developed a deep liking for young Joe.

Joe remembered Charles Gray with deep affection. From Gray he got his first book learning about birds and animals, and he guided Gray through the marsh, exploring with him the many Indian mounds and searching with him for arrowpoints and artifacts in the newly plowed fields. Gray explained many times what the state hoped to do on the marsh; to restore it to its original state as a habitation for birds and wild animals, to bring the water back onto the marsh by the construction of a dam at the village of Horicon on the Rock River, to try to entice the migrating ducks and geese to stop at Horicon, and to help perserve the great flock which traditionally flew the Mississippi flyway. They came directly downriver to wintering grounds in southern Illinois, where the game laws were very lax, and many thousands of birds were slaughtered, and sold commercially.

Gray had said that a stopover at Horicon might help preserve the flock, or slow the hunting down further south, and give the state an opportunity to contribute something to the restoration of a famous wetlands and the saving of waterfowl. He foresaw great research programs of banding geese, as Jack Miner in Ontario was doing, and new methods of managing wildlife. Hunting would be strictly controlled, and Gray foresaw a time when a hunter might only be able to take one bird in a whole season. That time was inevitable, he said, because the number of hunters would increase and increase.

Joe's eventual employment by the state seemed a very easy and natural development. One day Gray told Joe that the state had made its first land purchases. Farmers in some cases weren't happy about the state coming in to develop the refuge. First of all, Gray needed someone who was well acquainted around the area to help in the land acquisition problems. He had, he said, a lot of confidence in Joe, and if Joe would be interested there would be a continuing job for him in state service. Joe accepted. He had thought some about going to the university at Madison, but when the job came, he gave up that idea. From the minute he began with the State of Wisconsin until he retired four years ago Joe had never known a moment's unhappiness in his work. He wished now that Gray was around. Gray was a man who understood feelings without needing to describe them. He understood, and maybe that was why he and Joe got along so well, because Joe didn't describe things verbally much either. He felt deeply, and maybe Mary knew some of what he was feeling, but nobody else did.

Gray owned thousands of books. Joe had often been in Gray's home in Madison, and Gray showed him many rare volumes, almost all relating to wildlife, to exploring, to state and local history. Gray had been gone a long while, and there would never be another like him. The whole marsh development would never have happened if it hadn't been for Gray.

There were so, so many things to remember. Joe's thought at the moment was about Mary, and how he had asked her to marry him and come to live on the marsh. She was a girl from Madison, the capital city, who worked as a clerk in the Conservation Department. Gray had helped them meet, and when it looked as though Joe was going to be a permanent employee, his courtship of Mary became serious. She married him the week before they went to live at the marsh, not in a house at first, but in an apartment in a private home. She shared his enthusiasm, always had, though she didn't go often into the marsh. She encouraged him in the first of his pet projects, a project which was something more than the state expected of him. Joe could see, in the development of the country around the Horicon Marsh, that the wetlands were almost weekly becoming less and less. The farmers, after all, were chiefly interested in raising crops, and if there was a chance that they could reclaim a wet section of their farms by drainage, they wanted to do it. They were restless, and they had to be, or they wouldn't be productive farmers. Joe convinced a considerable number of farmers who had wetlands on their property that they could profitably start muskrat farms. If you can start an animal farm in Wisconsin, with the serious intention of raising and caring for wild animals, the animals belong to you. Coon, otter, skunk, beaver, deer, muskrat, and wild birds are all applicable under the law for game farming. The Wisconsin statutes were and are almost a model, and they enable an environment to be kept in which wild animals may flourish.

For two dollars a rod a farmer could get his marsh ditched to make a fine environment for muskrats, and a constant nesting site for wild water birds; and it made a sort of race track, to the embarrassment of the nesting birds, for coons and skunks out looking for eggs. Joe got a number of farmers in the area to create small, personally owned wetland refuges, and as one result, the farmers almost entirely swung over to a greater regard for conservation. Joe worked often along with them in their marsh projects, and the friendships he made then he considered the deepest he had formed in the area.

Joe also helped to actually buy from the farmers some of the land occupied by the Horicon Marsh. The state had small amounts of money to spend on land. The court had ruled that a wildlife refuge could not be established unless the state actually owned the land on which the refuge was to exist. The federal government, which was also buying land at the upper end of the marsh, had money, because the federal government had the revenue from the duck stamps, which were then sold for a dollar each. But such funds as the state could raise went to buy land only occasionally, and Joe made the original contacts with many of the farmers. The anger of many was still real to Joe. He remembered the muttered threats, and the statements that "the state had no business buying farmland." He was never told not to get out of his car as the specialist from the state office in Madison had been; but the land buying was never easy. Once in a while, when a state man from Madison had tried to make personal contact, the air was let out of his tires, and water drained from his radiator. Gasoline tanks were sometimes filled with mud. The whole thing was unpleasant. But it would never happen again, because the state now owned the land on the south, and the federal government owned it on the north.

Strangely, although no effective programs were immediately started to draw the Canada geese, the movement of the flock to the Horicon Marsh began shortly after the land purchase. Joe could see clearly the scene on a morning after he had returned from the war, with himself in a boat on a small lake near the marsh area. He had been hunting ducks that morning, and had had poor luck. The shotgun lay across his knees, and he was lost in a sort of thankfulness that he was back home; that his wife was waiting for him with breakfast; that the sun was beginning to show, and was turning the fall leaves an indescribable, glorious mixture of oak red and maple golden. The gun was loaded with number seven size shot — very light, but all right for ducks. The gun, he remembered, belonged once to his father. He'd given it to Joe in a kind of silent ritual between a father and a son, when the father passes to the son a priceless gift. The gun was a twelve gauge, double barrel, with hammers, and was in the same perfect condition Joe's father had always kept it.

He heard the sudden sounds, not knowing for an instant what they were. Then the two Canada geese came over, very low, honking as they came. For some reason they did not pay attention to the man in the boat, and as they came, even though he was aware of a strange reluctance, he threw the shotgun to shoulder and with two shots, killed both birds.

Later he carried the birds home and Mary came into the yard to inspect them. She held the birds, stroked them, and they both admired their beauty.

Then Mary had said suddenly, "Well, if you want them to return so much, why did you kill them?"

And he hadn't been able to answer, for there was then no need to hunt geese to control their numbers. The birds were dressed, cooked, and eaten. Neighbors were asked in for a wild goose feed, and the occasion was a happy one. But Joe never forgot Mary's words. For a long while he neither hunted nor killed any other Canada geese and worked harder than ever to make the marsh a place to which they might find food and refuge.

And as the years went on, he worked equally hard to provide for the hunting programs necessary to control the flock. He acted as a warden for many years. But his feelings now had finally jelled; the life of the goose had become the ultimate reality. When he retired they gave him a permanent key to the gates of both the federal and the state ends of the marsh. He could go and come as he pleased at anytime. And often he and Mary set out for the marsh to go way in, to sit quietly, neither speaking, just listening and watching.

Among the great flock in fall, Joe felt the poetry overwhelm him, even now. Thrill was too calm a word for what happened. He only knew that once in a while, on a late fall evening before freeze, when the sun is low and seems to be sinking into a misty world of its own, the marsh is lighted by a wondrous shaft of light which strikes suddenly across the ditches and comes to the very heart of the looker. Then the feeling of the wild all comes back again, and the primitive people are there, and the drum of wings in the whole sky is there. It isn't difficult for the wilderness to be recaptured at evening; it is a question of sky and lighting and the mind of man which expands into eons of past time if the conditions for such expansion are right.

In the days of the 1930s, there were very few Canada geese on the Horicon Marsh, Joe remembered. It was amazing, how, over the years, with the thousands of birds that continued to come, a belief evolved that the great flock had always stopped over at Horicon. It wasn't so. It was the way Gray wanted it to be someday, but he had no idea that the marsh would ultimately come so remarkably into its own. Well, the water levels had had a lot to do with it, and, to Joe it was remarkable that they had even been able to get the water back on the marsh.

The morning in 1934 when Gray said to him, "Joe, we'll close the dam at Horicon tomorrow. Back the water up again," Joe foresaw trouble for he knew the tempers of the farmers on the fringes of the marsh.

"They'll blow out the dam," he had said to Gray.

And Gray replied, "It'll be your job to see that they don't. The water has to come back."

And Joe guarded the dam every night, all night, for many nights, sharing the duty with another Conservation Department man. There were local threats, and one night men had come sometime after midnight and had tried to lay a charge at the west end of the dam. Joe heard them, and recognized, in dim lantern light, one of the men and called him by name. The man was one of the German farmers whose families had settled so plentifully around the marsh in the 1850s and 1860s. Joe called to him in German, for Joe's ability to speak the language of his mother was one of his values to Gray. Harsh words were exchanged, and a threat made against Joe's life. He stood firmly against the men, and finally they went away. It was the last attempt they made to dislodge the dam. But the bitterness remains even now, yes, even today. Joe knew

that he could find farmers who reviled the state, and who would gladly see every Canada goose in the world consigned to die.

Well, they didn't understand. It was like the killing, and the disappearance of the buffalo from the Great Plains; if the geese weren't cared for, and the marsh prepared as a refuge, if men were allowed to do anything they wished with the birds, then the great flock too would disappear — just as the passenger pigeons had disappeared. You had to prepare the way, year after year, and stick with the work, with the whole idea that wildlife in America could return, could be saved in the face of the vaster populations, the creep of the cities, and whole changes in countrysides where once ducks and geese, for example, nested and thrived in uncounted vast numbers. The plow and the herds of domestic animals were the doom signals of millions of waterfowl over whole prairie areas. Once there were lakes, ponds, potholes, and unbroken prairie — all suited to wild water birds. No longer. All was agricultural, all broken by plow, all bent toward the economic activities of man.

Thoughts like this were one reason why Joe had become a sort of recluse on his small farm at the marsh's edge. Here he could see man's activities dynamically devoted to the saving of wildlife. He could watch the struggle go on everyday, in and through all the seasons. The water on the marsh for commercial gain had failed. Now the state men had it their own way pretty much, and they could manage the marsh in the way best for the birds.

Joe had loved all parts of the activity. The mission, for it came to be increasingly recognized by him as a mission, became clearer as years went by. The geese, as they returned to the marsh through programs of feeding and protection, became almost his children. He felt emotional about the flock now; and he could hardly bear to know that it was time for the hunting season. There was one gander particularly that Joe used to recognize because he had a slightly damaged leg that gave the bird a curious twisting walk. He watched for this bird each season, and for several years had always found him present when the birds returned from the north. Indeed, Joe had thought that the bird also recognized him; and once or twice the gander had let him come very close. But then one fall, that was the year he'd retired, the gander hadn't come. Joe worried and wondered, but the bird never again appeared. It was the cycle of goose life, Joe supposed. Eventual death from a load of number two shot, or from a foe, or maybe just from old age. Death from old age wasn't so likely for a wild goose; but that could happen, too. And there were mated pairs that Joe recognized and felt attached to. He wondered whether he could recognize their offspring; but he never did, really, after the first season when the family still clung together.

Joe developed a program, too, of trying to care for the wounded geese after the hunting season. Usually there were many of these cripples, and Joe experimented with special feeding pens for them, only partly successful, for the healthy birds were not that concerned with the welfare of their wounded brothers and sisters.

There were several hundred acres of land that had to be cultivated each spring and fall, planted for the geese. They had exclusive rights in the refuge cornfields, and in the fields of winter wheat and buckwheat. As he worked longer and longer at the marsh and held a variety of jobs, Joe became a senior employee; he became the field supervisor, in charge of the farming operation. Looking back, he believed he had proved himself in working the land in the best way possible, so that it would produce the most grain for the birds. Some managers, maybe, wouldn't have gone all out in refuge farming. Joe did. The ground was always carefully worked, plowed, harrowed, and seeded with grain that had the best chance of producing larger harvests; for when the geese arrived, the cornfields and the green fields with winter wheat and buckwheat and alfalfa had to be ready. Now there were nearly a quarter million birds that stopped over at Horicon Marsh. The first arrivals of the flock always landed on the water and rested a little before they began to feed; but in a day, perhaps, they were flying into the refuge fields, and stripping the fields of grain with unbelievable speed. The marsh farmers always hoped there might be enough food to keep the birds until they moved south in November. But this was not the case. Sometime in October, late in the month, the refuge grain ran out; most of the green pasture crops the geese cherished were picked. The geese must now go into neighboring farmer's fields to feed. This is where the trouble always started.

One evening, Joe had been shopping in one of the small towns located around the marsh and was on his way home when he passed the cornfield of a farmer he knew well. The man had made threats against the flock many, many times, but had never, so far as Joe knew, taken actual action against them. But passing the field on this evening, Joe thought he saw a dead goose in the ditch and stopped his truck to look. He found, in the ditch and at the edges of the field, more than twenty geese apparently freshly shot and left to lie where they had fallen.

There was an investigation, of course, but nothing ever came of it. No proof of intent to kill the birds could be proven; but Joe knew that there were a lot of farmers who, if they could get rid of the geese pirating their fields by killing them, would probably gladly do so. It was a problem that had no real solution. The flock simply worked out from the refuge in concentric circles, feeding upon available grain, and staying in a field until the grain was stripped. Farmer's fields, or refuge fields probably made no real difference to the flock. It was only the grain that mattered.

There were, of course, some farmers who had made a very good thing, financially, out of the geese, renting hunting blinds, providing food and liquor to hunters. And there were other farmers who appreciated the birds for what they were, and hoped that their crops would survive. There were a lot of sides to the problem, but Joe knew that he would always be on the side of the wild birds.

It is almost impossible to describe what it is like to be alone in the early morning on the edges of the marsh.

In all of the water-world of the wild goose, there is mystery.

I suppose a lot of my life has been dreaming of what will become of this place.

Joe wondered sometimes, when he was all alone out on the marsh in the early morning as he was now, whether the birds, the wild geese for example, had any knowledge of the way they were, the way they looked, the grace they portrayed in flight, the emotions they inspired in man. He assumed they did not, any more than any other living form in nature had any idea of the effect of its form upon man. Yet man had been making poems about wild things for thousands of years, drawing pictures of them — even primitive man did that, and working the forms of live things into religions and traditions and beliefs. Joe supposed that the forms of the wild birds became what they were simply because it was more convenient for them to fly more rapidly, to handle themselves more practically in the air, to have developed through adaptation and necessity the way they were. But what puzzled Joe was the effect of the way they looked, upon people. He was always trying to compare the things that wild animals, birds and insects did to the things people did. He thought about it a lot: the way ants made their way over rough ground, going as fast as they could, with seeming purpose, and getting somewhere definitely the same way a man set off across a field to do an errand, to drive cattle, or for any other reason. And Joe was sure that the ant had no sense that he was covering any particular distance the way a man set out to cover a furlong, or a half mile, or a mile, knowing about how long it would take him to cover that much distance.

Insects and birds didn't do it that way, he guessed. They set out to cover some territory, but he didn't know that they had any frame-work of time and distance. The way the Canada geese took off on their migratory flights, they knew, from memory of having been there before, where they were headed; but they didn't know how many miles it was. And thus the goose wasn't necessarily impressed with the great distance he had flown in a night, or day. It was just that he was in flight, doing it in a traditional way, and finally getting to where he wanted to be.

Joe guessed that the way birds behaved and looked had something to do with the way he felt about a reality of God. He didn't know for sure that there was a God; about all Joe knew was that he appreciated the way things were. If birds didn't behave the way they did, didn't look the way they did in flight; if the marsh didn't appear in its many changing guises; if the sky did not change; if there were not insects behaving in the way they did; if he could not see the emergence of leaves, of spears of growth through the soil; if he did not sense the rooting of insects and birds and animals to their cycles, and to their homes, their environments, then his view and appreciation of things would be diminished. In the morning he was content to wait and to listen. It was as though there might be a thousand gods, or one, it didn't really matter, since everything was of the same fabric of being a part of, of liking, of silently accepting.

Well, the geese were certainly a part of the many-sided God that Joe thought he was beginning to understand.

Who was to say, really, that the birds did not also appreciate things? That they might really have some kind of inward response to the way water looked in its many moods. The artist, the painter, caught the ducks in flight; Joe had been struck silent by the power of certain artists' wildlife paintings — wild ducks coming in for a landing on a wild and gray morning, or geese bursting up from a field, the way he had seen them do it so many, many times.

The way people thought about God worried Joe sometimes. To Mary, God had to belong, finally, in her church. Her religious life was built around the idea of God being in a building, or a shrine, or in an institution created by men for God. He couldn't tell her how he felt exactly, and he probably wouldn't try if he could. She had her way and he had his. And she did love the wild things and the outdoors and nature. But when Joe was indoors and was asked to put his mind upon a God that existed as an overriding Being above all, apart, and still a part of, determining the way things were and the way birds looked in the sky, he found this hard to understand. He could, as on this morning, alone, quite well understand the many, many expressions of God, but God to him didn't belong in a human dwelling, or a habitation created for Him.

It was elementary philosophy, Joe admitted. And he knew that Mary's pastor could demolish all his arguments and feelings in short order. He would never attempt to argue about it anyway. It was pure feeling with him. He guessed that he had created his own church in the marsh, and that by coming out alone on an early morning, he was, in a way, coming out to worship and to celebrate in a kind of ritual.

Putting it in one way, he believed in the traditions of things — the habits that made animals and birds and insects behave in the ways they did behave. It was wonderful to Joe that these patterns of life had been established. They were predictable and yet, at times, they were not exactly predictable. You could guess from experience how birds would behave, and usually they did behave that way; but once in a while one came along that didn't quite fit the pattern.

The rituals of the wild, developed through thousands of generations, were the viewed things from which Joe gained the poetry he could feel and the God he could appreciate.

When he had first started to work at the marsh there were still quite a few Indians living around the area. Some of them were old men and women; they were descendants of Winnebago peoples who had long, long ago found the marsh a plentiful and constant supplier of food. And Joe had heard some of the old ones tell about their beliefs — about the birds, the sun, the way the world was made. It was myth with them, stories. The birds and animals were actors in the myths and stories. And the old people believed. They simply believed, and the myths and stories became real.

That was pretty close to what Joe felt about things himself. To the Indians it was simple legend created in a fantastic world in which they were very, very close to their god, or gods. Joe wished that the Indians hadn't gone away, for they belonged in the marsh and were naturally a part of it in the same way the birds and animals were a part of it. There was nothing artificial in the way they reacted, or the needs they fulfilled.

Gray had once told Joe that he wished the old Indians had been able to remain at the marsh, as it was in early times; for to the Winnebago tribe the marsh was their great place of ritual and food. But the Indians had vanished. Now, Joe knew, there were no Winnebagos at the marsh at all. They had disappeared, displaced first in the last century, then, little by little, the ones who had drifted back were also displaced. Joe remembered a day many years ago when he had sat at the marsh's edge with an old chief. The old man had sadly described the fate of his people. Joe listened, fascinated, as the old man spoke, for it was as though he were describing the end of the Indian's world.

"Winnebagos are not like other men," the old chief said. "They came not from the east; they are the only children of the Great Spirit. He put them on one side of the great waters, and his two great lights on the other. He gave us the buffalo, the moose, the elk, and the deer, for food; and their skins he taught us to use for clothing. He filled the waters with fish and covered the land with choice fruits. All these he gave to us; and he marked with his finger between us and the great lights, that we might not approach them. Upon the other side of us he placed a land of winters, where no Indian could live. After this the Long Knives (English) came, not as enemies, but as friends. They took our bows and gave us guns; for our skins they gave blankets and calicoes, and they gave strong drink to our hunters. They enticed away the young women, and when the Winnebago went after them they would not come back. Soon the hunter got lazy, loved strong drink and died. Many, very many, died so. Then it was that the Great Spirit told his oldest child, the great chief of the Winnebagos, in his sleep to leave the country to the Long Knives and cross the great water to a land nearer the great lights, where no white man had gone.

"We went forward, found a good land where this river goes into the great water. For two moons we found plenty of game and saw no Indians. We thought the Great Spirit had taken them all away to make room for his children; one morning we found the river full of canoes and Indians for one day's ride in length. Our chiefs and old men held a talk, and a canoe was sent to the strangers with as many men as there are moons in a year. They carried presents of wampum, fruits, sugar, and meat. These never returned. Their pipes of peace were thrown into the river, and their mangled bodies were hung upon the trees. Dogs were fastened in the canoe dressed like the Winnebagos, and the bark, with these, came down the river to our villages. Our good chief, seeing the tears of his warriors for their friends who were slain, struck his foot in wrath upon a solid rock which sunk in to his ankle, and called his father, the Great Spirit, to witness that the tomahawk be unburied with the Foxes, Sacs, and Chippewas, until a tree should grow from the place where his foot then stood. He then burnt a council fire in sight of his enemies and put blood upon the trees that they might see more was soon to be wasted.

"When they saw this, they fled up the river to Winnebago Lake. Our warriors followed — a battle was fought on its banks, which we lost, as part of our fighting men were deceived in the long grass by their guide. The Winnebagos, being swiftest on foot, gained this spot before evening. It was then the enemy's town, and they soon came, with their prisoners, little thinking we were here. Finding us in their town, they kindled their fires upon all sides and sent word that the next day they would eat the Winnebago chief. With the dawn the fight began. We soon drove the Foxes down the river, but they went round and joined the Sacs, who were above us. The rest of that day all was quiet, but the next night, at the rising of the moon, they again came out from their hiding places. This fight did not stop for three days; and we lost ten men for each day and night of the year, before it was ended. On the third day our chief fell, covered with wounds. While he still lived, he called his warriors to remember his wrongs; and with his own hands he pressed the blood from his wounds, which he gave them to strengthen their hearts. He lived to hear the cries of his enemies as they fled, and then, under this mound where he lay, he opened his mouth, and his spirit departed.

"In that battle the Winnebagos kept the town, and took many hundreds of canoes and many prisoners. These, except the young women, we killed. Those that escaped fled up the river, and the next day we pursued them. We came to the lake which makes the Fox River, and hunted for our enemy three days. Thinking the Great Spirit had taken them all from the country to stop our pursuit, we were about to obey his wishes and return, when we discovered a trail in the high grass. This we followed a little, when we came to a strange river (the Ouisconsin) running towards the Father of Rivers (the Mississippi), into which they had put their canoes. We now agreed to follow and fight our enemy until he should leave this stream and cross the Father of Rivers. At the Blue Mounds we fought them; and there we were joined by the Potawatomi, and they by the Menomini. At the mouth of the Ouisconsin they made mounds, and put their women and children behind them, for they expected a great battle. The Winnebagos had more fighting men than their enemies, but they [the enemies] fought for the last of their country, and the Winnebagos for revenge.

"For thirteen days the bloody strife did not cease, and hundreds of brave men fell on each day. At length the Great Spirit raised a loud storm of thunder, lightning, hail, and wind, which caused both parties to stop, for they thought the Great Father of all was angry with his children. The Winnebagos stood still, and their enemies all crossed the Father of Rivers, where they now live, at eternal war with our nation. No Fox or Sac meets a Winnebago (except in council) but one must die. All that great land between the Ouisconsin and the Mississippi is to this day disputed ground, and neither can safely occupy it. Winnebago, Chippewa, Fox, and Sac, all have country enough now.

"Sixty winters have passed over us since my father, who was then strong, told me of these deeds of our nation. But, my friend, the Winnebagos are not now wise. Once they had many thousands fine warriors. But every year we grow smaller. Too much our young men go into the white man's house and strive to live like him. They drink strong drink, and soon die. Traders buy our skins and give us strong drink, calico, and beads, which are not good for Indians. The skins of our game we want for clothes, and we could raise corn for ourselves were we left alone; but soon, my friend, we shall be no more. A few short years and our nation will be unknown. Then, when the stranger shall pass along here, and look upon the scenes of so many battles that have been won by the only children of the Great Spirit, and shall call out, upon every hill, where is the Winnebago? Echo alone shall answer from the west — 'where is the Winnebago!'

"Our enemies, the Sacs and Foxes, have grown strong and could now destroy us. They have shunned the ways and the haunts of the white men, and their people have multiplied. Their nations are large, and their warriors healthy and brave; the forms of our old men are wasted with age, and our young men are drunkards, like the whites. Our young women have become the companions of traders and boatmen, and our families are broken up. We are surrounded upon all sides by white men. We have no course left. We once owned the land where the two rivers run different ways (the Portage of the Fox and Ouisconsin rivers). But that is gone. The Winnebagos have no hope — they will no longer ask to live."

Thinking of everything that had happened that was seemingly wrong in the crowded white man's world, Joe wondered what the marsh would be like if the Indians had been able to remain, in an era not at all like the present. He didn't want to admit it, but maybe things would have gone better. But the Indians were gone forever, though occasionally Joe saw a few up on the highway watching the Canada geese. When he saw them, he wondered what they were thinking — whether they still had a concept of what the great marsh had once meant in the culture of their ancestors. Like the Canada geese who would forget if the traditions of their migration were broken, he guessed that the tradition of the Indians was permanently fractured, if not lost.

I've never been to that far north country, but I know the wild goose nests are there in the Muskeg.

I know the mother stands guard above her nest.

I know he watches for her, faithful forever.

I guess there are lessons to be learned by all of us.

Joe had quite a string of bullheads. He kept them alive and later would transfer them to a tank in his backyard. The early morning dark was merging into the coming day, and when the edge of the sun got a little higher, Joe knew that the fish wouldn't bite quite as well — longer between bites, anyway; but he had plenty for a mess and whenever he caught one he didn't care how long it was until the next. So, so many things to think about.

G. L. Wedge, for instance, and the far boom of hunters' guns made him think of G. L. — who couldn't stand to see anybody wound a Canada goose or a duck. At his resort he'd put a clothesline on stakes about a hundred and fifty feet from the firing line. Nobody better fire at a bird that was coming outside that line. The distance was maximum for a kill, and there'd be no far shooting on Wedge's place. That was over on Fox Lake, and with all of G. L.'s dedication to the welfare of the birds, he wasn't too happy with wardens, or for that matter, with officials of any variety. But a lot of the old timers weren't. The first time that Joe had ever seen G. L. was when G. L. and his son were skinning muskrats. Joe had trapped since he was about twelve years old, and he knew all the fine points of skinning muskrats. He also knew that the folks who lived on the marsh were very touchy people. They didn't want anyone tampering with what was theirs. Joe had come to the Wedge place just when the Wedges were starting to skin the rats, and Joe, without thinking much about it, just sat down and started to help them skin.

Well, they *were* touchy, Joe thought. Muskrat skins at a dollar apiece, or ninety cents, meant a lot to those fellows at that time. And the rats lying there belonged to them. So Joe was sitting there and got out his knife and started peeling off muskrats. He could feel the electricity in the air, too, for there he was skinning *their* muskrats. So for about half an hour the three of them just sat not saying much of anything. Joe didn't have to worry; he knew how to skin 'em. He was doing a nice job, not nicking them — and in those days it was a kind of common thing with muskrat skins — not so many trappers on the marsh now had ever heard of it; but then they used to run the skins through an old clothes wringer. It would squeeze the fat right out of one end. That saved you scraping the hide. You put the wringer tight on the spring and it did a fine job. Then you could put the skin right on the stretching board. And when Joe did that it broke the ice. Everytime he'd go back to see the Wedges after that he'd help them do whatever they were doing. It was an amazing thing to Joe, not so much psychology to it, though his daughter said he was a pretty fair amateur psychologist; it was just like a farmer. He was busy, maybe, and if you started right in helping him you'd make a friend. That was the way Joe got the confidence of a lot of people at the marsh; and it was why the state people in Madison liked him so much, and gave him the diplomatic jobs to do.

Joe received much in return from the Wedges. They were hunters, trappers, and fishermen mostly. They didn't care for town or for town ways. They lived in an exclusively male society; Joe could never recall having seen a woman at their place. They lived like bachelors, uncultivated most of the time; and the kind of men who came to the Wedge resort were the same way. No frills; grub, shotgun shells, game. That was it. But there was something else too. Joe had tried for a long while to figure it out, and sitting in the boat with the morning coming up made him think of it again. There was a kind of unspoken gentleness toward the wild — a never-take-advantage point of view with the muskrats, even. A lot of the trappers at the marsh in those older days didn't hesitate to spear muskrats through their houses. Take a metal shaft, sharp at one end, and thrust it down into the rats dwelling until you hit one. Sometimes they speared quite a few in a single house. But the Wedges never did that. What's more, if they heard of anybody doing it, they went personally and talked to the fellow. It was hard to arrest them maybe, but the Wedges took care of it in their own way. And if a hunter shot wildly at their place, or wounded a bird that was avoidable, or drank while he was shooting, that was the finish for him. G. L. took him aside, talked to him, and in a little while the hunter was out of there.

Only once G. L. had said to Joe, "Son, if the wild things go, if there aren't any more geese or ducks or muskrats or beaver — what would I do? My life would be over. I am half of whatever they are. Could you bear to see a sunset without the wild geese flying across it in the fall? Or never see the ducks get up off the marsh? Joe, will the time ever come?"

Joe had answered that he doubted that that time would come; but as things had gone, and so many, many more cars and people started to figure into the wildlife programs, and the waters got to stinking, and the fish died — well, maybe it could happen. The Wedges were gone now. Been gone a long while. Were there others like them? Joe sure hoped so.

Joe would do anything to help. He went to a farm onetime where an old man lived alone, and found the old fellow banging up some wood. That was what he called it — banging wood. Joe knew that if the old man didn't split wood he would probably freeze to death in the winter. There had been a couple of old bachelors that froze a few years before.

The old man got kind of winded, and Joe said, "Mind if I take a few whacks?"

And Joe knew, from looking at the old man's woodpile, that he wanted them split just so. Most wood splitters split the wood in four. This old man was splitting them in five, maybe because he got a little more instant heat, or maybe it was just that it was the way he wanted. *His* way. Joe thought he could read the old man's mind: he was thinking, "now this guy's going to crack them in four and that don't suit me." So Joe carefully split the wood in fives, and the old man showed him how to pile it just so, so neatly. A kind of work of art that Joe respected.

Joe had so many memories of the marsh — the fires that devastated the whole area. Nobody really did anything about the fires; and sometimes hunters or trappers who wanted the marsh burned off so they could see the muskrat houses better set the fires themselves.

They'd let the fire burn until the wind switched or until it hit a ditch — sometimes the fires would even jump the ditches. And even the farmers would burn the marsh at times to get better hay. They liked to get the old grasses burned out so they got the new, fresh carex and bluejoint. Joe remembered old Max, back in 1937 he thought it was, when old Max had been cutting hay on state land. Colonel Smith, who was the only attorney the Conservation Department had at that time, wrote to Joe that he would have to charge anybody cutting hay on state land a dollar an acre. Joe had heard the rumor, as it went from farm to farm, that old Max was cutting hay down near Quick's point. The bluejoint was very tall and thick down there. Joe went over there and saw the wagon tracks coming out of the marsh, and he followed the tracks right to Max's barn. Joe knocked at the kitchen door, and there wasn't any answer, so he went out to the barn to look around. He got a pitchfork and dug around on the top of the hay in the haymow, and sure enough, under a layer of alfalfa, he found marsh hay. He was still digging around when he heard Max's old car drive up.

He came over to the barn, and Joe met him at the door and asked, "Well, Max, what do you have here?"

"Why," said the old man, "that's alfavy." (A lot of old timers in those days called alfalfa "alfavy.") "You can see for yourself. Alfavy."

"What's alfavy?" Joe asked.

"Why, boy, alfavy's alfavy."

"Well, Max," Joe said, "the reason I'm here is that under this alfavy is a great big pile of bluejoint that you cut off the state land."

"You prove that?" asked old Max.

"Why yes," Joe said. "And if you'll get in the car with me, we'll follow your wagon tracks from this barn right back to where you cut it."

"Well," said old Max, "what do we have to do now? Suppose you want to go to court or something."

Oh no," said Joe, "this is a civil matter. You owe the state a dollar an acre."

"Well, that ain't so bad," said old Max, "though for the life of me, boy, I can't see why we can't cut the hay same as we used to. Nobody told us we couldn't cut it, until the state bought it all for the refuge. It ain't right someway."

"Max," said Joe, "do you like to see the birds come back in the fall?"

"That I do," said the old man.

"All right," said Joe. "And that's the reason the state has bought the marsh. So the birds will have a good place to stay, and where every hunter in Milwaukee and Chicago can't come and kill as many as he wants."

"Don't want them outsiders here," Max said, "but us marsh folks, we ought to be able to kill as many ducks as we want to. Ain't that right?"

"No, it isn't," said Joe, but he knew he couldn't ever make the old man understand how it was with the ducks and the geese. So he collected ten dollars for ten acres the old fellow said he cut, and let it go.

Well, anyway you looked at it, Joe thought, it was hard going with the local people in those days. It wasn't that anybody was lawless exactly, though there were plenty of young and old men who were known as "river pirates" or "marsh rats." They were an independent breed, very jealous of their right to hunt and fish. Most of them would have gone through fire to protect game from "city folks" or mischief makers, but they wanted everything the way *they* wanted it. Joe's role for the state didn't make him very popular. He was a sort of diplomat, caretaker, and warden, and when the locals found out that Joe could arrest them if he wanted to, the situation became far from a mutual admiration society. Joe got a couple of helpers after awhile, but the local folks still thumbed their noses until the wardens began to get a few convictions. They would appeal from Justice Court, and they had five days in which to appeal. Almost everybody arrested for a game violation would appeal, because most of them belonged to the strong local group called the Horicon Marsh Protective Association; and even if the culprit didn't belong, the members of the association welcomed him because they were all fighting the state.

Even when the state flooded the marsh, they had a terrible time with the dip netters. The local boys wanted to go on dip netting carp. They had always been able to dip net, and they saw no reason why they couldn't go on doing it. They figured that the state was interfering with their livelihood, because the minute the farmer started to quiet down his farm work for the winter, after the crops were in, then he started dip netting. After the chores were done in the morning, he would get out his dip net and start for the marsh. The farmers would smoke the fish, and pickle them. And in the spring, through the ice, the boys would dip net like crazy. They would take an ice saw, or a hay saw, and saw out a square in the ice and put their dip net down, and pull it up every so often. There wasn't any great rhythm to it; but they got fish. And in the spring when the northern pike were moving, the men would take all those they could. Pike is a little choicer fish to eat, and they felt that it was their God-given right to take just as many as they could. Well, Joe and his boys had a tough time getting convictions. It only took one bad one on the jury — they all had to find a fellow guilty; and most every farmer on the marsh or from the surrounding towns had some friends who exerted influence.

Well, there was the bad and the good. Joe recalled a day when he was out on the marsh with a reporter from a Milwaukee newspaper. It was a day in spring, sometime he thought in April, and the sky was light blue with kind of dusty edges, the way it looks around the marsh on an early spring day. They heard the geese faintly, and then saw them, very high, a tremendous flight that seemed to stretch from end to end of the marsh. The time was the late forties, and Joe, as he watched the geese peel off and circle down, thought it was almost like dive bombers, and he had seen plenty of those, too, during the war. The geese unwound in a circular way; they seemed to be coming right down on top of the reporter and him — a beautiful sight that Joe could never forget. There were only a few geese on the marsh before that happened, and it was like watching the first of the vast migration arrive. It was like a corkscrew, Joe said later to the reporter, the way they came down; and the radar that's built in them told them that they had arrived at the proper place.

Joe took the reporter, too, to a small meadow near a town called Markesan. The state had been able to purchase about ninety acres of the marsh there, to preserve and protect it. It was one of the very few places where the Maxima, the giant geese, come down in central Wisconsin. The marsh was on the Grand River just east of the town. The great goose expert, Dr. Harold Hanson, once told Joe that the place was like a "mirror image." From on high the geese look down and see something that they like — maybe it is their own reflection in the water. Anyway, whatever it was, Joe thought the idea of a great reflecting mirror among the sedges was a beautiful thought. He went there year after year, on his work of course, and then just because he loved the place. Usually he saw geese there.

When Joe had much to do with game protection, he could recall one of the first deer killed by car. Nowadays he knew that many hundred deer were killed by autos; but in those days a deer hit by an auto was unique. People take everything for granted — the way the deer have come back. It was wonderful and mysterious to Joe. He knew why, of course, simply because there was more food, probably more protection, and the deer moving south and south. But the whole concept of the proliferation of wildlife, the increases in numbers, was mysterious, too. The mystery came, he thought, partly from the fact that in the old days, back in the area, people hunted them firecely, no matter what time of year. Then, if a farmer saw a deer track, he got his dogs and his neighbors, maybe, and they set out after

the deer and stayed with him until he was dead. A deer was big news then. One of the first violations that Joe heard about was at Ashippin, in the great Ashippin marsh, below town, near the railroad. There they were running the deer down. To them it wasn't wrong; it was just part of living — the way things were. A wild thing was there to be dealt with by man as he saw fit, and to kill at anytime. They even hunted deer by horse and buggy, by railroad handcar if they could get one — anything was fair when the chase was on. The wildness affected kids and women, too, as well as the men. Joe had seen ladies out in the woods, trying to beat deer toward their men's rifles; or ladies carrying guns themselves, stalking, waiting as well and as patiently as any man. In the old days every boy had to have a gun as early as he could persuade his father that he should have one. And most every boy did have a gun — small bore rifles at first, or .410 shotguns, maybe, single shot, with a hammer, since the hammer guns were thought to be safer. Joe had bought his son a gun at age twelve and had taught him to hunt and to shoot, and if he had it to do over Joe would probably do things the same way. The kid had learned a great deal about the appreciation of wildlife from the gun, and what it meant.

It didn't always work out that way with kids. The Horicon Marsh edges were full of tin cans, beer cans, containers of all kinds, many of them holed by small rifle bullets, or by shotgun pellets. Some guys would shoot at anything; they preferred something alive, but if the live things weren't there, most any target would do.

It was like the stories about the thousands of adventure-seeking young men who went west in the 1870s carrying firearms of many, many varieties: pistols, single shot heavy rifles, shotguns, repeating arms, even old Civil War muskets. And the stories told how they would crowd the back platforms of the railroad cars and the windows, shooting out the train windows at anything that moved. The trainmen seemed to condone it, too, at least Joe had never heard otherwise. But his dealings with people around the Horicon Marsh at times (and usually not the natives) had made him understand how they got the buffalo, and why the millions of bisons disappeared, their bones piling up and being collected at the railroad yards by the bone hunters.

Up north of the marsh, Joe knew a fellow who had brought some buffalo to Wisconsin, and now had a nice herd of them in his big pasture. He kept them there, feeding and caring for them simply because he loved the way they were, and perhaps he, too, had read the stories about the buffalo hunters and what they did to the immense herds. It might be, Joe thought, his way of contributing to a debt that the American people owed to the buffalo and to the buffalo gods, whoever and wherever they were.

There were times when there were flocks of blue or snow geese at the marsh. They seemed to come in cycles, some years there would be none. Joe didn't know why — whether there were storms that moved the flocks sideways, away from the marsh, or whether there wasn't enough graze food, for the blue goose is primarily a grazer. Joe had seen the barred and white-fronted goose on the marsh; and he had seen the little blue heron, which was rare, and the green heron.

Joe remembered when the first biologists came to the marsh. At first they considered the scientists the lowest thing on the totem pole; up to that time the workers who had developed the marsh, built the dam, put the water back on, prepared for the migration of the birds — these were the ones who were, they thought, important. They couldn't see what a biologist could do that they were not doing. Yet, as time went on, Joe had obtained a second appreciation of the wild things from the biologists. He had heard about some of the things they were doing: banding the birds, investigating diseases, researching the plant life, identifying the wild birds, controlling the diseases among the muskrats — but Joe had never had science fitted into its proper place. He was ignorant, and he knew it; but he became terribly interested. He completely accepted the scientists; and then he began to listen with fascination to the stories they had to tell. Joe grew more and more impatient with the hot stove yarners, who spat and opined that no feller from a college could ever know as much about wildlife as *they* knew; after all, they had hunted the marsh for fifty years. The

colleges ought to stay out; just as the state and federal governments ought to stay out. *They* could manage the birds and the animals in their own way.

What the hot stove doubters couldn't ever understand was the dedication of the scientist — how these men and women worked tirelessly, stayed out in the brush, doing it the hard way; gleaning information which would make the birds proliferate, stay healthy, and be there when the hunting seasons rolled around.

Well, there was a pecking order among the men who looked after the refuges and cared about the welfare of the wildlife. Years ago the ranger was the king. They were the really first ones to be hired, so there were more rangers. Then the wardens came on the scene; in Dodge County, Wisconsin, if the state hired a new man and he didn't check in with the warden, well, his chances of having any influence were just about nil. The warden wouldn't let the fellow sit on the bench, even. When the rough fish crew came in to try and control the carp and suckers in the marsh, the warden figured that he was the supreme ruler of the marsh universe, and whatever he said they had better do. Well, it was hard for the rangers and the wardens to let go; but they had to. The fish and game managers finally got established in their rightful place. And last, of course, was the poor biologist. He got the crumbs. But it hasn't stayed that way. They have come to realize that unless you are a specialist, you're working blind. Joe had a greater and greater respect for the biologists and worked with them as closely as he could. In a way it made him feel that he was reflecting a part of their education, their knowledge. That made him feel good; for as he grew older he wished that he had completed an education. He would have loved the research and would have liked to be in the thick of it, not on the sides as a helper.

He wished that his father had been more respectful of education. Joe had actually wanted to go on to college.

His father had said, "Oh, what's the use, Joe. You can make a good living. You don't mind hard work, do you?"

And Joe hadn't minded hard work, only now he believed that he'd had a bit of a spark, a bit more feeling for nature than most of the local folks.

In his daydreams he wondered what he would have become if he'd gone to the university. Possibly he might have been able to continue research, even in his older age, after he retired — instead of just watching and fishing. Somehow, the geese knew what they should do, by instinct. But man couldn't really function that way. His instinct was too often faulty, and was emotional rather than the kind of inborn thing the geese had. Like the way they would let you come up close to them on the marsh, or out by the highway but never, when they didn't have the sense of protection. They knew.

The lore of the Canada goose, the flock, was what interested him most. And when the biologists came, they expanded his knowledge.

Spring hunting in the old days was common, Joe's friend Willard said once as they sat having a beer in Willard's basement. They all did it. The old hunters looked forward to spring because it was a good and a pleasant time to kill ducks and geese. Of course, after they caught onto what was involved, then nobody hunted in the spring. They realized that the birds shouldn't be disturbed when they were nesting and raising families. But in the old days they didn't think much about that.

"Conservation is really a sort of new idea, ain't it?" Willard said.

"Yes sir, I remember too, how those dead geese looked, all piled up there on that muck. I saw 'em, and nobody really reported it. When the water was drained down there were dead geese in there. Lead poisoning it was. Yes it was, call it whatever you want, it was lead poisoning. They just come in there and gobbled up the goldarned lead and used it for grit. In some places all that lead, those pellets from about a million shotguns, doesn't affect the birds — where there is hard bottom on the marsh the shot doesn't settle down in the muck. You see, what really happened was that before they put the dam in down here at Horicon, they raised the whole marsh by having the water high, and the bogs all floated. Yes sir, the whole bottom of all the grass and the peat and all that just floated up to the surface. Sort of like floating islands. Why, I seen them put a line on a floating island and pull it with a boat. Yes sir. The action of the water just pounded the bog all to pieces. That water was black with muck and the bog, all over the marsh in the spring of the year. Now the bog has come back after they been drawing the water down, but it's come back so fast that you can't hardly go duck hunting. You can't get in and out of the channels. Years ago, when they had a dam on the Horicon Marsh at the west side — in fact they had two dams — they maintained the places where these fellows were shootin' — like the Diana Shootin' Club and the others, they had certain areas where they hunted. That's where the lead is. Now you take on the marsh where these people go skiing — marsh skis that is — that don't mean nothin'; but it's in the old channels where they used to go years back — that's where most of this lead is.

"Now look over here at this old map. It was drawn years ago. And here we are now, at Horicon; then you go up — this was before the main ditch they dug with that barge in 1912 — they used to go up along the old river, then over to the Four Mile Island — and where the old clubhouse used to be out on that point, there's where the lead is. Those old hunters dug a special channel up to their clubhouse, probably dug it with oxen. They could push right out in here to what they called the Mieske Bay and Mieske's River, see? Then they would go up in here to this place they called Big Lake. That was another good area to hunt, and over to Goose Island; then they would hunt all over this whole area north, and finally they could go clear up to Waupun.

"I trapped over there this last fall, over around where the old Diana Clubhouse was, you know. I went over there one day. There wasn't any snow, and I just poked around. But they covered everything up with a bulldozer when they tore the old club down, and I don't know why they ever did that. There wasn't no foundation to the club so there's none of that to see. It was built on stilts, you know. Now I tell you, once my dad and a few of the fellows here in Horicon controlled Steamboat Island. Was a building there. We tore that building down, but we left the stone part stand. We had a steel door on there and I had the key to it for years. Finally give it to a guy and say for him to put the key in the history museum. Don't know if he did or not. Had to have that steel door on Steamboat Island because they kept a lot of furs in there. I don't know why they tore the Diana Clubhouse down. Maybe it was because old Mieske died, then Burgess got hold of it — that was his uncle. He got control of the Mieske farm, and after that that whole thing went to pieces. The state got ahold of the land, of course.

"Now when they started to get a flock of geese at the Horicon Marsh, it could have been in the early fifties. Wasn't much before then, that was sure. A few geese and flocks now and then. They brought a couple of hundred goslings up from southern Wisconsin, and started a flock on the marsh. We never had any permanent stoppers like they got now. They fed this flock of captive geese, kept 'em pinioned, and in a pen; a certain part of that flock stayed here. But I heard that a golden eagle got some of those first ones. Killed about nineteen at one time. Some of those geese nested on the marsh. I guess some got away and migrated too. And hunters must have got some of them. But they drawed down some other geese, too, and the wild ones would feed right there in the same places. I suppose that's what started the big flocks comin', because a goose, he will remember where he got fed, and he'll come back to that place.

"These younger fellows, they don't know anything about anything. My old partners are dyin' off. We talk a lot, us old ones who are left, about the times we spent on the marsh. I tell you, that old marsh has got a strong pull. We talk sometimes about how we tried to make a livin', in times of the depression, and how we had the game wardens chasin' us. Actually, we didn't hurt anything; we didn't cost the state any money, and I believe we did a good job of conservation, too. Somebody had to look out for the muskrats and the birds — somebody who knew something about 'em.

Why, some men the state sent up here didn't even know when a muskrat fur was prime. We made a little money on the marsh, too, dip netting carp, or choppin' out mink or spearin' rats. We caught a lot of mink in there, but they ain't there like they used to be. The water's too high. The only time they'll come back is when it freezes over, and there's rats. Then they'll come back and dig into the hills. Otherwise, well, a mink is good in the water, but he don't care about gettin' his feet wet all the time. I seen 'em when they get their feet wet, to set and shake 'em.

"Well, we was considered bums by a lot of folks around here, because we loved the marsh so much and sometimes went huntin' on Sunday. But some of us are worried now. We don't know how they are ever going to disperse that flock. And just letting hunters kill the birds, that's not going to do it either. I know how it can be done, probably, by not planting any more corn on the marsh. No more. Just plant winter wheat, because the goose is a grazer. He will eat off the green, and then his manure is such good fertilizer that they can raise a better crop than ever — wheat. But not corn. Of course it would kind of shift the burden onto the farmers around the marsh, because I guess the geese would go out there to get the farmer's corn. But maybe the farmers could do something about it then — well, that ain't a very good solution, is it? But something's got to be done or all them birds will die sometime. A goose plague.

"Tell you what happened when they was fighting so hard to bring the marsh back for wildlife. Curley Radke, he was the leading conservationist, and he and others prevented us from trapping on the marsh for ten years. Wanted to bring the rats back you understand. Well, we did some trappin' anyway, on the sly, but we couldn't do much, and you know what? The rats all died off. There got to be too many. Got a disease and died. The rats were just dyin'. I could go and pick up more'n a hundred a day, and finally the state says to us, we'll give you thirty-five cents apiece. You bring 'em and put 'em on a pile. We'll pour gas on 'em and burn 'em up. Well, I got many everyday. Just took a pitchfork and heaved 'em on the pile. I got in trouble from doing it, because I had a sore eye, and some of the meat from one of them rats hit me in the eye. I was lucky I didn't lose the eye. Overcrowded. That's what was the matter with the rats. They got to crop 'em off. They know that, too.

"We had great fishin' here too, until the state started the rough fish removal. Then it wasn't any good after that. Reason was that the fish crews would leave the rough fish in the traps until they were dead. Then they'd just open the gates and let the dead fish float out — why, we stacked the dead fish up like cordwood down here by the dam. I got pictures showing that. They were trying to get the carp out all right. Their intentions were very good, but they were killing the game fish too. They got 'em all in there together. That was about 1936 or 1937. After that our fishing hasn't been any good, except for bullheads. Lots of them. Friend of mine over here, he catches hundreds, knows just where they are."

Joe spent a lot of time with old friends, men who had trapped and hunted and lived on the marsh all of their lives. Visiting was one of his main pleasures, exchanging reminiscences, and when he wasn't at home, Mary knew where to look for him — at some old friend's house, or in one of the taverns. And when he was alone, thinking of many things and searching through his life for the meaning of it, as he did so often now, he was always recalling the comments, often rambling, but fascinating, of his old friends. The conversations were like floodgates at a dam, opened, so that the water could pour out and over, and Joe at times had trouble remembering just who it was said what. Yesterday, though, it was George who had done most of the talking, because Joe had taken a stranger to see him — a fellow who wanted to know about old days on the marsh. And when George started talking, he moved right along. The stranger had started it by asking George about eagles — had he ever seen any eagles on the marsh?

"And yes," George replied, "in about 1954 there was one bald eagle up here by the Coleman's fence. Yeah. But the bird was gone after that. Me and Harold McTighe, we watched him quite a bit. Harold had one arm. The eagles always sat on that one tree. They lived on field mice and stuff like that. Whatever become of that eagle, I don't know. I figure somebody shot him; I know Bill Shoemaker shot one. That was years ago, on a farm at Iron Ridge. And when Bill come to town and brought the eagle, it had a wingspread of eight feet. And that time there was no law. Could shoot an eagle anytime you could find one. Bill shot him in the woods on his farm.

"In nineteen ought six I was ten years old. My dad was kind of a watchman at the Diana Shooting Club, and I'd go up with him to club rats and spear rats, and like that you know, see. We got half the rats. Never got any pay or like that from the club. And then I went with him, after school. That was my hobby, going in the marsh. I'd spear rats, and when I met my dad by Four Mile Pond I'd maybe have three or four rats. He maybe had a dozen. Rats were payin' about, oh, ten, eleven cents apiece. That was a lot of money. That was more money than my dad made in the shop. In the shop there they were getting ten cents an hour, for a ten-hour day. They thought my dad was a millionaire when he got all them rats up there. But rent them years was three or four dollars a month, you know. And when you bought butter you could get that for about fifteen cents. Lard was maybe five cents, like that you know.

"Dad was a house painter and we run short of money, you know how it was them years. Dad says me and him got to go up to the Freeman Slough and spear some muskrats. So we got three rats and we sold them for eleven cents apiece. Old man Boston, who run the tavern, was a fur buyer. So I had thirty-three cents, and it was like I was a king. We bought some butter and lard, and a gallon of syrup. A whole gallon for five cents. They would pour it out of a barrel, and let it run into your bucket. Thick and good. On pancakes, that was livin'. That's a good many years ago, though. They talked about dredgin' the marsh as early as 1907, and took them a long while to get ready. They built the dredger up at Oakfield. Was about nineteen ought ten or eleven or twelve when they dug down through Horicon digging out the river. I remember, because me and dad painted the bridges. There was the long bridge and the short bridge. The short bridge was down by the Catholic church. We moved the bridges off and we painted them, so we wouldn't have to work over the water. Could see the fish! In them days we never lost fish like we do today. I tell you what they got now. They got this here dam open again. Why open it this time of the year? Winter? All the fish, when the water is running, will swim upstream as far as they can go. I had a friend up at the federal end of the marsh there, and he says thousands of perch were laying up there dead. Then the dead ones wash down when the dam is open. Years ago we always burned the marsh off; then it was dry, and the fire burned peat and all and it purified everything, you know.

"Now they sometimes burn on top of the ice, the dead grass, but the manure from the geese is on the bottom. So what good does that do? You try to educate them guys that run the marsh once. I tried to tell them, and tell them, when to burn the marsh like in the old days. Oh, they says, that will kill too much. But the fires didn't do permanent damage, just cleaned everything up. I tell you, we used to take a team up to Quick's Point, that's where the state headquarters is, and we could go right up to the Cotton Island, Four Mile, and then on up to Skirmish Line, that divided where we could cut hay, because beyond the Skirmish Line that land belonged to the farmers; clubs didn't own all the marsh, they was just leasing certain parts of it. The Skirmish Line was just north of the Four Mile Island. That's where the boys used to hunt, just where it come around the bay, you know, right on the point. The Skirmish Line run across the marsh, east and west, on the north was Mahlzahn's Bay, and the hunting clubs shot there. But when you get down to Kekoskee River, they had nothing to do with that. Now the state and federal governments, they have bought it all up.

"The old club men, they hunted about everyplace. They would push out from their clubhouse on Clubhouse Island over on the west side of the marsh — they had a special channel over there — and they'd push up to Swan's Neck, then into West Lake, then to Mahlzahn's Bay; and if they wanted to go the other way that would be a long, long way around, clear down by the dam. I could draw a map of that, easy, the way it used to be. Here they got everything balled up. All wrong. They don't know what's what on any of them new maps. But I know what it was like before the dredges was here.

"In them old days we started out from here, Horicon, then you had Freeman's Slough, then you went around by Mieske's you know, Max Mieske had a lot of land there; then comes One Mile Island, they you went around by the three willow trees — they stood there as long as I could remember; then you went around to Schuster's Hole. Fellow name of Schuster used to hunt there. Then you went to Coleman's Fence, and from Coleman's you went to the old Diana Dam. Then they had one channel where the mud dam was. They built a dam out of stones and mud; the main dam, that would take the branch over from Cotton Island and through there — Stony Bay Bushnell's Knob, West Lake, Four Mile Pond, all that. On the other side, you had Mieske's River, then you go way up to Mieske's Bay. It goes through there to Steamboat Island, that channel there. Then you went up to Apple Island. Then you'd got up to the south of the Big Lake, then you had to go up to the forks. That's as far as the club men went. Then the two ditches there, one went to Struks and the other went to Waupun. In there they had a place they called Rice Lake. For us to get on into there we had to leave Horicon here at the south end of the marsh about twelve o'clock at night in order to row away up there before daybreak. It was about six miles from here up to the dyke, if you go around them channels. That's a long row at night. And we had all DePere boats. Maybe you don't know it, but under them boats you had runners, so in the spring when we trapped, we had our push paddles with pikes on 'em, and you could shove right out onto the ice, just like a sled. Them boats are light. You had to have runners, how could you push a boat? You'd ruin the bottom.

"You would balance yourself and push with this push pole. Like I said, it had a pike on it, made in a blacksmith shop — a kind of rounded prong on each side. Man you could shove that boat, it'd go like from here acrost the street. Them poles were made of most any kind of wood, ash wood was best. Still the guys would break 'em if you don't know how to handle 'em. You never must bend them. Always push straight.

"The vegetation grew pretty thick in the marsh. But we knew the channels and we knew where them holes was. You would go over to Steamboat Island, it was a high island, and you could stand up there and look over and see where the birds was hiding. You knew where the holes was — the Four Mile holes, the Cotton holes. When we went to the Four Mile Island, there was the Four Mile, the Baby Four Mile, and the Cotton Island, but they don't have that on the maps. Before you got to that Baby Four Mile there was a channel going in there called the Sauerherring Slough. I tell fellows that and they say, you must have been crazy.

"All I cared about when I was young was wildlife and baseball. Instead of going to shows and like, I'd rather go up in the marsh fishin'. And now when I am old the thing I like is fishing. Hunting I can't do, because you can't hunt. In the old days you would go up there and see a duck, you looked, and you shot that duck. Now they shoot and then they look. They ain't got no hunters now. I call 'em 'hunterinas.' You can't use no decoys now. These fellows shoot all the way from here to Madison, just to fire off the shells. But I do trap some rabbits when they come in to eat my garden. They will eat everything if I don't trap them in boxes. Except I don't trap when they got young ones. The season is closed then. But when I trap the rabbits I take them up to the State Headquarters. They take the rabbits out on the end of Quick's Point — out there where there are about a thousand foxes. They eat the rabbits right up. Does that make sense? And you can't hunt there. You can't go there. You can't do anything there. I go up there raise hell with them guys pretty near everyday. When I was planting pheasants they would come right up to my door for food. But I can't plant them any more. Because if I do a hunter will come along and shoot one, and if I walk out and tell him he can't do that, he may threaten to shoot me. Right here in the city limits they will do that. One year I got eggs from Poynette and

raised a lot of birds. And I planted 'em, and when they was growed they all wanted to cross the tracks. When they got over there, it was private and I couldn't even go to check on 'em. Fellow wanted to shoot me. You see how that works?

"A lot of Canada geese have nested on the Horicon Marsh — the ones they started and raised in the pen. They had a bunch in there once, I heard they got from southern Wisconsin someplace. When I trapped in there, we had to stop doin' it in the spring, and then I would find these goose nests on a rat hill. There would be six, seven, eight eggs. The way they put the geese in the pens, and kept them for awhile, that helped bring the geese back on the marsh; the ones flying over would see the ones on the ground, so they'd stop. When geese hatched on the marsh, then they came back here, too. I don't know, if I was a goose, that I would stop much at the Horicon Marsh now, the way they got the hunting arranged, and I guess I wouldn't if I was a hunter, either. You pay ten dollars to use a club blind, and then you can shoot one goose and you're done. Now you can go down to Hustisford, and you can shoot one everyday. Now that isn't fair. I know guys that shot as many as fifty geese down there. Up here you got to have that tag and one goose only.

"But there is this craze for killing. I know where maybe fifty deer hang out around an orchard. They ain't safe anytime. Shining deer, killing on the sly — and if there is a Hungarian partridge around, well the farmer's wife she has a gun too, and she will go out after that bird. The kids'll all have a gun. The old man'll have a gun. The dog'll have a gun in his mouth, yeah, that's how it works. I remember when Emil Mieske raised prairie chickens. Must have had five hundred. They was running all over. When I was trappin' in nineteen twenty-two or twenty-three, there was a whole flock of Mieske's birds come along. I had an automatic gun and got six, six that Emil never got. But he had guys go in there and shoot them birds, too, and he got paid for that. And he should because it costs a lot to take care of that stuff. But it's just like a pheasant. You can't plant a pheasant and think that pheasant's going to stay. He's not. He's gonna go, unless you feed him all the time. They'll never stay all the time in one place. What are they killing all them blackbirds for, down south there? Me and my wife will go up here on the hill, and we'll just set there and we'll see lots of blackbirds. I like 'em. I lived off them for a long time when me and dad got froze in on Steamboat Island. The ice wouldn't hold a boat, wouldn't hold nothing. We had to stay there, and me and my dad, we shot blackbirds. We'd take the breasts and the legs, and we put 'em in a little soda and salt; you have to have that stuff when you're camping, you know. Then we'd go to work and fry 'em. Finest thing in the world.

"We seen a wolf one day, big, and he run acrost in front of our car. We got some wolves in here all right. I told the guys up at the state headquarters about that. They says, you must of been dreaming. But we seen it, through there, east side, where that woods is. And one other time we seen one, when we was going to Juneau, in that brush. Big bushy tail. Used to have beavers in here, too. Was here until onetime the water went down and killed 'em all, killed the whole works.

"Onetime me and another hunter, we was trapping and we found about four hundred geese that was dead. That was all muck, and these geese was in there, in that stink, and they ate that. And the men at the marsh, they says they would send the dead birds down to Madison and they would find out what killed them. I says you don't have to send them; it was lead poison that killed them. I knowed what it was. I trapped in there. Took the scientists three months to find out I was right. All that lead shot in there, enough to sink a ship. But that's the way it is. State is like that. When them guys cut a muskrat hill open they kill all the rats; that's all right. When I do it, they call me an outlaw. When they do it, it is an error. When I do it, it is a crime. That's somethin' I don't like either. All that muck and that crap and everything, about *that* thick, you know. That's what is pollutin' the water now on the marsh. You should never open them dams until you get some good rains, then wash it all out of there. That manure acid is all coming through and it is killing all them fish they planted. This flock of geese in there — how many? Two hundred thousand? They make an awful lot of manure — man, oh, man.

That acid was so strong when I trapped in there you could take a metal tag — you got to have a tag on each trap. That tag would get as small as a pinhead, would just eat that metal right up; that water — you can smell the acid. It's worse than a sewer. That's true, you ask any good trapper, he will tell you the same.

"What I think will happen, mister, is that they are saving those grand birds, and it has been a success. But they are savin' them, and suddenly them birds are going to get a disease and then they will all be gone. The works — like the passenger pigeon. There are just too many geese. It will be death for the birds, and no fun for the goose hunter. Like duck huntin', they got a point system. You can only shoot one of this kind, or that, and people from town, they don't know what they are shootin' at. They shoot at everything, and that's why there are so many dead birds just left out in the marsh. If you just said, hey, you are allowed four ducks, I don't care what kind, it would be much better. My dad was one of the best trappers and hunters ever was on the marsh, and he was one of the best shots, too. Now, if these guys see a duck, they will all shoot at it, because they want that duck. Hell, a lot of 'em never even take the duck home. If they see somethin' comin', even if it is as far away from here as Mayville, they'll shoot at it. Just so the other guy don't get it.

"Now they dug these new ditches up there on the federal, I don't know if you seen them or not — the river away up past headquarters, and then on up to Inermuhle's Island, see. I fished in there a couple times, and I got some of the finest fish you ever see. I'm a big bullhead fisherman, see. But the refuge guys chased us out of there. I don't know why. But I will get in there, though. I'll see Bill Proxmire and Gaylord Nelson. They will help me. I go fishin' though, anyplace along here around Horicon. Right by the bridge, I ain't gonna tell you what I tell the other guys; but I go up by the bridge and the old icehouse, then I go down to Riverbend Park and the Juneau Clubhouse. So I come in with a nice string, and the guys say, hey, where'd you get them. Where? I say, hey, you know where the dam is down here? Well, I didn't fish there. That's the way you got to tell 'em, you know. You tell one guy and you go there the next night they'll chase you out. There'll be a million guys there. Remember that now. There are a lot of bull-heads. Last fall I had my neighbor up here, and I got a big tank out in the back here where I keep fish alive. I says, well, I got sixty of 'em last night. Damn lie, he says. Come here, I says, and he stands there starin' into the tank. Can't believe his eyes. Where'd you go, he says. I says, come along. So he went along. Used two castin' rods. I says, Herman you got to have a fishpole. I says, there's grass in there. Your lead weight is gonna go down in that grass and you can't find it — you gotta have it just so that weight hits that grass, a little above that grass — well, that night I caught sixty and he got four or five. The next night he was there, with a pole, and he caught sixty. Then he was there day and night, see. Well, there you have it. Yeah.

"Bullheads is the best eating in the world. I ate 'em three days after they had all this water treated, you know, all that poison to kill the rough fish? Didn't hurt the bullheads, though. I fished down there, and a German fellow come along, and he says, what're you catchin', and I says, carp. Oh no, dey poison dem outta here, he says. I says, naw, I'm catchin' bullheads. They killed 'em all, they killed 'em all, he says. I says no they didn't. Come here once. I give him a look at my pail. My Gott, he says, I gotta come down tomorrow. See how that works?

"But now they opened these dams, and you ain't going to catch nothing. The minute the dam is open the fish will swim upstream. That's why we got so few game fish and perch right now. They go up to the federal marsh, and when the water goes down, these fish will die; then they will all come floatin' down here. Well, the Public Service Commission down in Madison, what they say goes. Most of the fish are goin' over the dam from the Horicon side, carp and stuff. But we had a lot of northern pike when we had carp, and you never see too many of them die, until they monkied around with these dams, here; just when they shouldn't open, they got it open. They open it and close it, open it and close it. Fifteen times a year. They should leave nature alone. Let it run over the side, slowly. Carp is a good eating fish, too. My wife can cook 'em so you can eat bones and all. The worst sow pig you can get, that will eat anything, I mean, is that sturgeon you get up in Lake Winnebago. They eat any darn thing that's rotten. And the carp, he'll eat anything that's rotten, but the northern is different. Two kinds of pike. My dad never called a pike a pike. Always pickerel. I come home one day with a northern that weighed about twenty pounds. Where'd you get that pickerel, says my dad. That's no pickerel, I says. Who says it ain't a pickerel, says dad. Well, I says, Doctor Forbes, he is a guy that studies that stuff, he says it is a northern. Northern, says dad, hell, it looks like a southern to me. That's the way them old timers was.

"And onetime I brung home a walleye. I says to dad, hey, I got a walleye today. And dad says, walleye? What is that? Well, he only had two fish, that was a pickerel and a pike. The walleye was always a pike to him. A northern was a pickerel. And he give me a slap in the mouth. If they'd give the carp a different name you would see how the public would go for them.

"Well, you gotta be real mean if you want to live long. I trapped that marsh in weather when them other guys wouldn't even go outdoors. I was in my sixties then. Well, you got to have a good line, too. But I can't do nothin' alone. I know how it ought to be run all right. When I was married fifty years, Bill Proxmire, he writes me and says, anything you want, or anytime they won't give you what you ought to have, you let me know — like fishin' or trappin'. Last fall I was married fifty-five years, November the sixth. But why should I celebrate that stuff for?"

A man can't look down when he is around geese.

You have to let yourself go.

If you give yourself to the goose, there is freedom.

Faith on earth is faith in what's up there.

God is up there with the birds, that's for sure. I don't really know about His being down here.

To me the wild goose must be a favorite of God.

Joe often toyed with the idea that the Canada goose might be a lot more intelligent and perceptive than anybody guessed. All you had to do, Joe considered, was to watch the way the birds knew so, so much about their environment — the hatching places, the refuges, even the specific boundaries of the sanctuaries. Maybe they actually saw and kind of understood a lot about the world of people. Joe liked to think about the things the wild goose saw as he flew south from the nesting grounds in Canada. His thoughts usually started in the old, old days, before the country was settled by white men. When there was only wilderness, solitude, mirror lakes and clear streams, forests unbroken, marshes wild, with perhaps small bands of Indians camped on stream or lake. The Indian women would be, in season, harvesting the wild rice, floating in canoes and grasping the long stalks, bending and beating out the heads; or harvesting the wild berries. The men would be creeping upon the deer, or the wild bird. Their harvest was small, and the flocks weren't depleted much. Yet there was a balance. Man didn't occupy the position of being the chief determiner of the size of bird flocks and had nothing to do with their management.

Now how was it? As the wild goose flew south, what, indeed, did he see? He saw the timber mostly gone, small patches of woods, and large sections of cutover lands growing again to maturity. And within the timberlands he saw the flashing signs of many commercial enterprises: bars, amusement spots, restaurants — developed to serve and to bring the tourists into the remaining "American Wilderness." The goose saw the spread of the habitations of men — the flinging out, the encompassing, the sprawl into valley and hill of many houses, of dump yards of junk accumulated through seventy-five years — never moved, never covered. Wouldn't the wild bird, the free one, have some recognition of change? Wouldn't he sense the waste, the abandoned automobile bodies, the spew of man's general litter and spoilation? And the cities themselves, pinacles of human development, what of them? The goose could not see within the dwellings, or within the towers of business, and so could not know the troubles of the city, the conflict of races, the plight of the poor, the disappearance of trade. He saw only the city sprawl and the ugliness of it by day, and the mystery of its endless lights at night. He could see the unbelievable linking of the highways that sped into the cities and out again, circling, one upon and over another, and the land where the highways ran, once the land of primitive people, now placed into an immutable fetter of concrete.

And the streams and the edges of the lakes — the edges of the lakes were green and ugly to view from high above. All around the lake edges were the habitations; at times very close to one another, each habitation with a little wharf or pier jutting a few yards into the water. And upon the jutting wharves people were gathered, as though striving to find sun, wind, and water and almost as though this were an impossible task; whereas the goose remembered when water, sun, wind, and land — were there open and free for all.

And what of the upper air itself? Often the goose on the wind must struggle for his breath, gulping into his lungs the fumes of smoke, or the rising smog from a half-million dwellings and automobiles. Maybe the goose knew the terror of life below, Joe thought. The battle that every man now must make against the machine, against the thousand implements, some strange to his hand, not at all like the stone knife, the copper knife, and the stone axe of the primitive Indian peoples. Nor did the goose understand, because he was essentially still of the wild, the enslavement of people to the routines of their lives, to the necessity of gain, the tyranny of family. And especially the goose did not understand, having great wings to beat the air and transport him, the automobile, and what it meant to man in man's native world.

The goose knew, perhaps, that the automobile was a factor in the fear he felt at hunting time. For most of the hunters arrived at the shooting grounds in automobiles. The goose saw the endless lines of automobiles on the concrete highways making their way slowly on Fridays and Saturdays, and back again on Sundays. The men moved swiftly. Sometimes more swiftly than the Canada goose. And indeed, much, much more swiftly in the airplanes that the goose often saw above him, and sometimes below him in the skies.

Ah, thought Joe, the goose is the meaning of the wild. But what is the true meaning of man's world, which is never wild at all. Man seeks the goose, because man wishes that the wild were once again his. He has killed the wild but he also desires the wild. When he kills the goose it is perhaps a ritual to recall the wild, or to sacrifice to the gods of the wild.

Such ideas bothered Joe and occupied a lot of his dreaming hours. He could not see how it could possibly end, or be resolved, this terrible dilemma of man. The wildlife refuges might be a small part of the answer, for Joe had seen how the people came eagerly to the refuges to view the birds, to rededicate their lives, perhaps. But the refuges were only tiny islands and could never, never possibly serve all the people.

Joe knew that philosophers at the universities were grappling with these problems all the time. Maybe they would find the solutions. On Joe's simple level, the problem appeared to be unsolvable. There remained only the essentially wild, the birds who had not really become tame, for they still followed their old, old traditions. Man fed them now and tried to help them; but aside from and despite all this, the birds remained a free thing, and it was the free thing that Joe believed might lead to the salvation of man.

One winter, Joe kept close track of a pair of Canada geese that actually wintered at the Horicon Marsh. He had often said that if a goose could get food and water, he could survive even a very cold winter. The pair had made no effort to leave the marsh, and Joe presumed that one or both of them had been wounded. He never did know whether there was actually anything wrong with them or not; but he assumed they had been wounded. He had, in the late fall, noticed them, together and slightly apart from the remnants of the flock, most of which had migrated. The pair kept showing up in the feeding areas long after all the other birds were gone. He made an effort to put shelled corn out for them, and they came and took it and disappeared into the marsh. He never saw them fly.

He was fearful that predators would take the pair as winter came on, and he watched for them day after day. For several days in December, they did not appear. He presumed they had been killed. But just before Christmas, they appeared again at the feeding place, and Joe brought his young daughter to see them. The pair let them come quite close, and the girl gave them names, Betty and Jim. Joe didn't understand why she picked out those particular names, but the girl said they fitted a sort of happily married couple who *would* have names like Betty and Jim, nice people, she said, and able to take care of themselves.

Joe didn't want to tell the girl all the hazards that faced the geese during the winter. Cold, of course, but that might be the least of it, if he continued to feed them. But there were worse menaces. The foxes hunted the marsh continually, and the red fox comes silently through the cattails, over the frozen muck, and he might take a goose unawares, and with flashing teeth sever into the neck or break it with a sharp twist, never letting go no matter how the bird threshed and beat its wings. Joe could see the tragic action, the mate fleeing, terrified, to wander alone in the grasses, while on the spot where the attack was made there were feathers and drops of blood, and the raccoons could take a goose, too, though not so easily perhaps as the red fox, but efficiently enough if the bird were hurt or could not fly, or use its wings to help it along the earth.

Each evening Joe's daughter would ask if he'd seen the pair of geese that day, and sometimes Joe had and sometimes not. On the days he didn't see them, he made up many excuses why he had not; the birds were resting out of the wind; or they had gone for a journey to another part of the marsh. Perhaps they had found other food to eat, and he was sure they'd be back the next day.

In late February, the geese stopped coming to the feeding area altogether. He was sure then that they would never see them again. He inquired around among the other men at the marsh. There was no sign. One of the men told Joe that he had rumors of a couple of coyotes in the area at the west side of the marsh. He thought that very likely the coyotes had taken the birds. They could certainly have done it with little trouble. Joe didn't tell his daughter anything about the coyotes, but he kept a close watch out for them. There had been some coyotes around the marsh area of late years.

February went, and halfway through

March the birds had not appeared. Joe never did find out where they had gone to. He assumed they had found food somewhere — a place where the snow was thin and the stubble of corn had some grain on remaining cobs. But one day he was walking along one of the open areas where the river widened. The ice was still strong, and far out he thought he saw a moving object. As he came closer, he could see that it was a pair of geese, and he muttered, "Betty and Jim," and walked toward them. He had to come around the end of a point of the shore, and as he emerged again, in sight of the birds, he saw the eagle. He hadn't seen many eagles at the marsh. There had been some several years before, and then they stopped coming. Now he watched as the eagle dropped down on the geese. As he came down, they flattened themselves on the ice; the eagle missed and swooped upward, circled, and came down again. This time, one of the birds flattened on the ice and the other beat the air with frenzied wings. Again the eagle went upward. He circled just above them and dropped again, claws stretched down and out. The geese seemed to be waiting for him, and as the eagle came down, one goose, the gander, struck out wildly with beating wings. One wing caught the grasping attacker a slight blow and knocked him off balance a little; but the eagle came back instantly to attack. The other goose, neck stretched out and one wing beating, fled across the ice, and Joe could hear her high, terrified honks. He decided that he must interfere, and hurried across the ice toward the birds. He heard the eagle scream, and the wild honking of the goose, and it looked to him as though the gander had decided to stay and fight it out, for he actually faced the coming foe, neck stretched out, and Joe imagined that the bill was open and that the goose was hissing defiance. The eagle came swiftly at the goose, and as he came upon him, the goose flapped strongly and a wing caught the eagle across the body, a full, sturdy blow. The eagle was knocked sideways, slid across the ice a little way, and came back on its feet. Joe yelled then, and the eagle left the goose and strongly flew upwards and away. The goose, too, spent no time thanking Joe, but took off after his mate, wings flapping, and crossed the river rapidly. Joe thought perhaps he would not see the birds again, but he was happy to be able to tell his daughter that he had seen them, and that they were safe.

He thought a long while about telling her the story of the eagle; then he decided that he would, for it was, he thought, a very interesting tale, and the goose actually came off the winner. He didn't think what might have happened if he had not been there to help the goose. He imagined that the eagle would have attacked again and again until he got his talons and beak into the goose, and that would have been the end.

When he told the girl, she listened eagerly, and when he related to her how the goose had fought the eagle, she said, "That's what Jim would do. He must be the bravest goose in the world."

Joe did see the pair again. In April, one of the marsh workers told him that he had seen a gander swimming near a small island at the west side of the marsh, near the opening of the old Burnet Ditch. He thought there was perhaps a nest there, because he saw another goose briefly on the shore, and then she had disappeared while the gander swam rapidly back and forth, giving short, warning honks. There were, occasionally, some geese that nested at the marsh, only a very few in these years, though Joe remembered that the old Indians had told him there used to be many birds that did nest there. Joe took a canoe one day and paddled slowly over to the vicinity of the island. It was then in June, and Joe spotted the gander swimming near the end of the island. The bird disappeared around the end, and from the shore, trying to follow him, came the goose, and behind her, five goslings. They swam easily, though they were quite young, and Joe murmured, "Well, Jim and Betty made it. They lived to have their family after all."

The little island where they had reared their brood was well chosen, far enough from the main shore to prevent predators from swimming easily out to the nest, or to take the little goslings. A mink could easily have done it, or a great horned owl could have captured a gosling easily; but apparently they hadn't, and the foxes and coyotes couldn't get at them at all. Again Joe marvelled at how well nature protected its own. He thought about how he would get great pleasure in telling his daughter about the family that Jim and Betty had produced. And he only hoped that he could tell her that the goose family had all flown away in the fall, down to Illinois with the rest of the flock.

Joe had been often saddened and shocked by the callous killing of birds on the marsh. No matter how strict the care taken to protect them, someone every year slew several blue herons. Joe had come on them every year floating in the waters of the marsh; and one year he had seen twelve slain ones all in the same area. He could not fathom why a person would wish to kill herons, or bitterns, or indeed, sand hill cranes, for these too he had seen killed in the area.

Onetime, in a marsh adjoining the Horicon, he had stumbled upon a sand hill crane which had been wounded. The beautiful silver grey bird, with pink feathers on the head, had been shot so that it could not fly, but it fluttered and stumbled in front of Joe and was still so elusive that he could not capture it. Eventually he called another warden, and together with the help of a fisherman's dip net, they caught the bird. They took it to Joe's house, and for a little while had it in Joe's living room. The tall bird stood in great dignity while they discussed what to do with it. The wound did not appear too serious, and they thought it could definitely be saved. The Milwaukee Zoo seemed the most likely place for it to recover, and Joe drove the bird to the city in the special crate they improvised. Later, when the bird had indeed recovered, it was returned to the marsh and given freedom.

Joe never really saw more than a few giant Canada geese at the Horicon Marsh. The bird, which is a subspecies of the Branta Canadensis, called the Maxima, the big one, or the great one, rarely if ever stops over at the Horicon Marsh. The big birds are vastly independent, wary, and like very much to keep to themselves. Their nesting patterns are individually theirs; they fly, in a sense, their own flyway. Joe had secret ideas from time to time about trying to raise a small penned flock of the giant birds as he knew the Inman family were doing in southern Wisconsin, but he never did. Often, though, in inspecting the flock as it rested at Horicon, Joe tried to imagine that this bird or that one, was a Maxima.

Hunters have always been out to get the "biggest," or the "strongest," goose in Wisconsin and so far as anyone knows it was a giant Canada taken by a great hunter, Jim Robar, in southern Wisconsin. The hunter had waited patiently for days and days, matching his skill, his knowledge of habit and of tactics against those of the great goose. And finally, he was successful. He outguessed the goose, waited in a place the goose perhaps thought the man would never be and bagged him. The wingspread was nearly eighty inches, and the weight more than eighteen pounds.

This old gander might have been a leader of the flock of giant Canadas which winter at Rock Prairie in southern Wisconsin. He, without doubt, had seen much in his life, which was probably quite long, for the life of the Canada geese is lengthy if they escape hunters, and disease and predators, and probably other hazards. One Canada goose is known to have lived seventy-five years in captivity. In all those years, a goose could grow pretty large; and the stories of large geese in the old days probably came from the fact that there weren't so many hunters; geese lived longer and were therefore larger. The giant goose could have been eight, ten, twelve years old, maybe older, when he was shot. He had a mate, of course, and they had nested in the wild country east of Winnipeg a hundred miles, where few other geese nested. When their brood, which might have been somewhat smaller than that of ordinary Canada geese, three goslings maybe, instead of five or seven, was ready, and the last food disappeared from the north, and the ice had formed on the rivers, the Maxima and his family set out for the south. They would winter in southern Wisconsin, farther north than other Canada geese, for the Maxima is a very hardy and very, very strong bird. Not only does he weigh about a third more than an ordinary Canada goose, he is probably tougher all through. He is the greatest and the best. Thus he can stay in the far north longer than other wild geese. He would, prehaps, remain in the far north all winter were it not that he can get no food.

The family, joining other Maximas, flew directly, one hop from the Canada nesting grounds to the Rock Prairie. They had been coming for generations; nobody can remember the prairie in a time when there were no giant geese there. It was their special place, their American home.

All the way down, of course, they were aware of hunters and avoided the places where, traditionally, they had been harrassed on previous journeys. They also flew very high with great speed. The rate of travel was at least fifty miles an hour. If the wind aloft was at their rear, their rate picked up and they might fly seventy or seventy-five miles an hour, great wings beating, necks far outstretched, pointing, pointing, never erring in direction; the leader, observing, perhaps, the landmarks so well known, and flying south by instinct too, by sun, by wind — who knows how and why the wild goose flys, and how he keeps direction?

Joe knew, as he sat alone in the boat, that he would never have been satisfied with a pen of giant geese, just to watch in captivity. The thought of the wonderful birds free, high, independent, was the great thought; but how wonderful it was, too, that now so much was known of the bird, and that real protection could be given. Much of the knowledge was assembled in Wisconsin.

The giant Canadas are the only flock of geese in the state that winter in Wisconsin. They spend the entire winter, from the time of their arrival the first week in November, until they depart sometime the third week in March usually. The entire flock at Rock Prairie is supposedly composed entirely of giant Canadas, and was sometimes said to be the only flock of these large birds. The giants are scattered however all through the West and the Midwest. Much more is known about them now, of course, largely because of Dr. Harold Hanson of the University of Illinois, who reidentified the subspecies as the Maxima, and discovered several substantial flocks. Also, the goose raisers, the interested and well-meaning folks who collect and raise pens of wild geese for reasons of research or pleasure, have been much attached to the Maxima. He is so much larger, makes a better show, and somehow, once in captivity, seems to take easily to a sort of domestic life.

Originally the Maximas were the birds of the prairie region that stayed on the prairies until they were displaced by the settler who came with his ever-present plow. The settlers destroyed the environment of the Maximas. They hunted them assiduously, too, for a giant Canada, well prepared and roasted, is a delectable dish for a pioneer family which might well have been half-starved. The marshes, the water holes, the prairies themselves, were sys-temically changed, made into farms; and the wild birds, especially the wild, wild Maximas, simply departed from the prairie states to the wilder, safer locations in the northern plains states and southern Canada. They nest much farther south than the other Canada geese, and they winter much farther north.

Not every Maxima weighs as much as the great gander shot on Christmas Day, 1925, by the skillful hunter in southern Wisconsin, but where an ordinary goose weighs six, eight, ten pounds, the Maxima may weigh ten, twelve, even sixteen pounds on upper limits. They are magnificent birds, and watching the flock at Rock Prairie take flight is to experience a thrill of beauty and power. Seeing them in flight takes one back to the time when they were absolutely free over wild prairies, unbroken by man and one understands a little better the feeling of the American West when it was wild, unsettled.

Scientists say that possibly the flock of Maximas is declining, and that it has been on the decline for the past twenty or thirty years. Efforts have been made to discover why, and to recommend practices of management which will restore the flock to its normal size. The hunting mortality is very high for the Maximas, which is probably the chief reason for the decline. Everybody wants to get one of those big geese!

Up north, in the nesting grounds, too, the black flies take their toll of the goslings. The black flies are cruel pests and will attack almost any living thing. They attack and bite the goslings, and they carry a disease, which is like malaria, and which kills quite a few some years. Other Canada geese are not necessarily exposed to this danger in other nesting areas.

Rock Prairie, where the Maximas winter, is an agricultural region. When the early settlers arrived in that part of Wisconsin, they found wide expanses of open land with some oak trees. The soil was deep and black. The land-minded settlers recognized the possibilities of the region and settled without looking further. Their judgment was correct. The prairie lands of southern Wisconsin became immensely valuable.

In such a tempting region, the wild had little chance of preservation. With the farmer came wheat, then corn. Substantial homes were built, and large families were the rule. Then came the cattle. Dairying became a leading industry; much roughage and grain had to be raised for the cows. Great barns were constructed, and then silos to hold the chopped fodder. The country became prosperous, but the prairie plants disappeared. Every acre was plowed. The birds, which nested upon the prairie, left. But some of the birds clung to the land. The giant geese, which had their homes on the prairie, stayed, and returned again and again. The settlers killed many with firearms brought in covered wagons from the east. But along Turtle Creek, in the bottoms, there was cover and water, for the creek was spring fed, and there were holes that did not freeze — in these places the geese stayed and survived. They fed along the creek and roosted on the water. There were formerly many giant Canadas on the Big Foot Prairie farther south of Rock Prairie, on the Wisconsin-Illinois border; but they were not protected there, and when the refuge was established finally at Rock Prairie, the giant geese moved there.

The local people, those who simply enjoy wildlife, appreciate the giant Canadas in their neighborhood. There are also a large number of hunters. There is a seventy-day season on Rock Prairie — open all day, everyday. The birds are hunted from the time they arrive in November until the end of the season. The hunters may kill one bird per day per man. If the hunter is lucky he might theoretically kill seventy geese during the season. This is really not possible, because of the wariness of the birds. The hunting pressure makes them extremely timid, and they become almost impossible to approach.

One of the better features of the Rock Prairie-giant Canada situation, is that there are not a vast number of hunters there, as at Horicon. The land is all privately owned. The only way a hunter may get permission to shoot, is to take a lease on a portion of a farmer's land. The state leases the land for the refuge from the landowners. There is thus no blind rental and there is no public hunting. The only public hunting situation is the "firing line" on Lake Delavan, nearby. Many birds use the refuge during the day, fly to Lake Delavan to roost, and fly back the next morning. When they fly to the lake in the evening and out of the lake in the morning, the hunters line up on the road by the shore of the lake and just hammer away at them as they fly over. They call it the "firing line." Even though they are larger in size, the Maximas are susceptible to gunfire, same as any other goose. Any goose has to be hit pretty hard to come down — a broken wing, or shot in the head, or through vital organs, but they can be and are killed. No doubt many of the large birds carry loads of shot in their bodies.

Hunters refer to the giant Canadas as the "big geese." Most of the hunters probably don't associate "big geese" with a subspecies at all. To the hunters the geese are just "big," bigger than usual. The hunters appreciate that they can hunt the big ones rather than the smaller Canadas. Some of the goose hunters will hunt any geese; but there are select hunters who have formed a curious affinity for the large birds, and feel much less satisfaction in hunting others. It may be, too, that the Maxima is a worthy antagonist in a period when goose hunting in many areas has simply become "goose shooting." The big birds offer a definite challenge.

One old hunter at Rock Prairie has been hunting this flock since 1929. He has many pictures from the old days, of two or three hunters with all the geese they can carry, and in the field behind them stands a Model T Ford covered with geese.

In the old days, too, it was possible for the hunter to use live decoys. The old hunter tells about the days when he had a "calling flock," and owned a very large gander, a very talented caller. The goose and the man used to ride to the hunting grounds together in the back seat of a friend's car, and as they went down the street the old gander stuck his head out the window and called to people as they passed.

Everybody seems to be interested in the "biggest and the best" of most anything, and the giant Canadas are the biggest and the best of the species. They are generally lighter in body color and they have a longer neck. During the winter their plumage is always in good shape. They are a very beautiful bird. Unfortunately for the general public, they come to Wisconsin at a time of year when bird watching isn't so pleasant. You can go on a beautiful fall day to Horicon and see two hundred thousand geese. At Rock Prairie, when the giants are there, the temperature is usually well below twenty degrees.

As far as their northern habitat is concerned, it is almost impossible to see them at all. They nest near the White Shell Provincial Park in Manitoba. The country is Canadian Shield country, solid rock, vast forests, pine, almost no marsh country, swift rivers and streams — not the type of place you'd expect to find geese. They nest, like the ordinary Canada geese, on small islands, or on top of beaver houses, or along the shores. The nearest town to the giant country is Rennie, Manitoba — pretty much a wide place in the road, few buildings, a cafe, a hotel, and a small grocery. The local residents either work on the railroad, or run small businesses or are associated with the tourist trade. A great many are trappers on the side. There are some Indians who move in during the wild rice season in the fall, but they leave again. Most of the hunting of the giants up there is accidental.

Joe recollected that it was Gray who had suggested in the late thirties that they experiment with a flock of geese raised right on the marsh. He thought it might have an effect on luring more Canadas there. When some of the geese raised at the marsh migrated, then they would, perhaps, bring others back with them to their native place. Nobody knew for certain how the plan would work; and some of the geese would be penned. But Gray told Joe he should try to find some young goslings and transport them to the marsh.

Joe had heard many times about a farmer in Rock County who kept a flock of Canada geese. It was about 1939, he thought, that he had set out one morning with Mary to drive to southern Wisconsin to see the farmer. The Wisconsin countryside that day looked especially beautiful — wide and slightly rolling fields — as they drove south from Horicon, through Watertown, Lake Mills, and south to Delavan. The crops were in, corn was coming up in tiny green sprouts, and fields were green with coming oats. The farms, as they drove south, looked more and more prosperous, and Joe remembered that he'd been told that the land in southern Wisconsin, in Rock and Walworth counties, contained the best agricultural acres in the world. The land flattened as they came closer to the Illinois line, and Rock County was prairie flat in its broad deep-soil character. When the pioneers came it was unbroken prairie, and the flatlands toward which they were headed had been named by the settlers, Rock Prairie, and south of that, Big Foot Prairie. There were small creeks that traversed the land, and the small timber and brush grew thickly along them.

That day in 1939, the Malones had found Foster Inman and his wife, Viola, at home, and extremely hospitable. In the old farmhouse, the Malones were given drinks of water from the clear, cold spring that flowed in the cellar; the overflow went out into the creek that Inman had dammed to make a long pond for his captive flock. He had many Canada geese in the enclosure, and the four, the Malones and the Inmans, stood a long while observing the birds and listening to Foster Inman's account of how his father had become interested in Canada geese, and had started the flock, and had so imbued his son Foster with the same interest that he kept the project going, and indeed, had plans for expanding it.

Foster Inman told, that morning, how one day in the spring a few years earlier the captive geese had started up a loud outcry. Until the Inmans had gone outside, they did not understand what the trouble was. Then they saw the large flock of wild geese circling above the small sanctuary. They behaved as though they might come down, and the Inmans were careful to keep back out of sight. The flock did come in and landed among the captive geese. Fortunately, Inman said, he had placed an unusually large amount of corn on the hillside, and the wild birds stayed all day, feeding and visiting with the captives. When evening came, the flock took off; there must have been a thousand, Inman said, and the captives watched them go, necks raised, looking very sad that they, too, couldn't join the migration. He went on to tell how a wild gander had come one year and had taken for a mate one of the captive geese. They were, apparently, very happy together; but when the migration time came in the spring, the gander became restless and always flew away to join the flocks heading north. In the fall he would return and live with his mate through the breeding season. Then in the spring he would leave. Inman thought this went on for several years. Finally the gander stopped coming. He had probably been shot, and his mate, the captured goose, seemed to wait and wait. Each year she had raised a brood of goslings.

Inman had many stories, and explained to Joe how the giant Canada geese had been coming to Rock Prairie for as many years as anyone could remember. The great geese seemed to have found their home in the prairie country and loved to linger through the winter in the creek bottoms where the creeks were spring fed and the water did not freeze.

The two hundred goslings that Joe bargained for that day took most of the ready young birds that Inman had on hand, the season's product of the captive goose mothers that had nested. Joe did not, of course, take them on that day; but after the negotiations with the state were completed, and the young goslings had been purchased, Joe and others came in a state truck and brought the little birds back to Horicon. They were raised by hand there, and in the early fall they could fly. They hung around the feeding places, often trying their ability to fly, and going farther and farther afield. They had had no experience with any other location now, and while a few, sadly, fell to hunters around the marsh that fall, most of the young birds did survive because they did not venture into outlying areas very much. Some were kept as captives.

When the flyway migrations went south, mostly overflying the Horicon Marsh, the young birds became very much disturbed, and one morning, the entire free flock sailed away, joining a flight that was passing over, very high.

Joe watched them go, wondering whether any of the young birds would ever return; but in the spring, in late March, about a hundred of the young geese showed up at Horicon Marsh. There they were well fed, for the men were by that time very much interested in the project. The young geese remained at Horicon for a month, until April, and then they disappeared, apparently heading north with the general flock as it flew toward the northern nesting grounds.

That fall the young birds, now reduced to less than a hundred, returned to Horicon. They appeared to be right at home, coming immediately to the feeding places where they had been fed before and mingling with the captives. And now there were small stands of corn for them left in areas within the marsh. The young birds went into the corn and fed there day after day. Joe noticed that a couple of the birds, ganders probably, were very good callers, and that, when wild geese flew over, these birds called loudly; and often the wild ones came down to join the small flock. In the first year or so the men at the Horicon Marsh did not notice much of an increase in the number of birds feeding; but the next spring there were definitely more. The small flock of young geese had been joined by about a hundred others. It was a small beginning.

That fall, as the migration came south again, and this year, after the young birds had mated, the flock was substantially larger. It now contained the young original geese and their season's offspring plus a few other wild geese attracted by the food at the marsh, and perhaps by some mysterious telegraph which made them follow the leadership of the young birds.

There was a lot of debate as to whether this small experiment was the real start of the Horicon flock which through the years became enormous. Foster Inman thought that it was, and the story became a stock one with Inman, who told it to practically everyone who visited his place in southern Wisconsin.

Joe wasn't sure how important the experiment with the goslings really was, for the small flock subsequently decreased, and it wasn't until after World War II that the wild geese really began to arrive; and in the 1950s, other experiments with captive geese at the Horicon Marsh had excellent results.

Through the years, Joe made many journeys to southern Wisconsin to visit the Inmans, and to exchange stories with a couple of great goose hunters who lived at Walworth. One of these men, Jim Robar, may have been, in Joe's estimation, one of the most skilled goose hunters and amateur conservationists of all-time. Jim, who had been postmaster at

Walworth and an avid antique collector, had been exposed to the thrill of goose hunting early in life. It became his chief hobby, and with his friend and almost foster son, Mike Krohn, hunted until his death. It was Jim Robar who had killed the largest Canada goose ever heard of in southern Wisconsin — the bird that weighed upwards of eighteen pounds; and Jim was fond of telling the story of his battle of wits with this great bird which he eventually outthought and killed.

That had been a fair contest; in fact, everything that Jim did was fair and sporting. He had told Joe many times about his effort in behalf of the Canada geese on Rock Prairie and Big Foot Prairie. During the winter he made almost daily trips into the countryside, making sure that the birds had food and that they were faring all right. They became his charges, and he was proud of their great strength and vitality, for the giant Canada geese wintered right through on the prairie. They did not go to southern Illinois as most of the Canadas did.

Jim had a hand in creating the Rock Prairie Wildlife Refuge, which was a State of Wisconsin project, and furnished a sanctuary for the geese. Hunting pressure became very great as time went on, and more and more hunters came to southern Wisconsin from the cities.

Jim Robar and Mike Krohn hunted every fall and killed their quota of geese, but they were impatient with sky blasters and casual and careless hunters. They considered themselves skilled professionals, and they thought of the goose flock as their greatest resource for sport and for beauty, too. Often they just went out and watched the birds; or occasionally they drove to the Horicon Marsh to watch the spring migration come in. They were helpful to students from the university who came to the prairie to band geese, for the migration habits of the giant Canada were not very well known.

One day, in 1974, alone in his small home, Jim Robar died. Joe Malone felt the loss very keenly, and not long ago Joe had driven down to Walworth. He and Mike Krohn sat together at Hall's restaurant at a country crossroads near a cornfield where Jim and Mike usually had their goose pit. Mike talked a lot about Jim and about goose hunting on the prairie, and about the special decoys they made.

They had their own way of making decoys. They knew that if they could find a material to stuff the decoys, something that wouldn't deteriorate, that they could make cloth decoys that would last practially forever. Jim was an artist and could paint the birds, and they knew how to shape them so that they had different poses. They finally discovered that sugar cane, shredded, was the perfect stuffing, for it would never decompose. They stretched the muslin cloth over a rough wooden frame, and with a stick, packed in the sugar cane tightly from the tip of the head to the tail. When it was stuffed, they closed the opening in the cloth and used an airplane waterproofing paint to seal the cloth. Then Jim went to work. He painted the birds so realistically that when a number were together in a field, they couldn't be told from the real thing. They made a lot of birds in Mike's basement, and Jim made some in his. Mike still has more than three score of the prized decoys waiting until he goes hunting again, if he ever does, for he misses Jim almost too much to go alone.

The hunter and death are a part of the life of the wild goose.

I have looked at them often along the barrel of a shotgun.

But, my God, the beauty when you are near them!

I could never disturb them for death while they rest.

They wait. Sometimes, it is as if they wait for me.

In the corn, they seek life and perhaps do not fear death.

I wonder if they discuss death.

What a store of wildness there must be in their hearts.

If I could only know all of their life story, the fantasy of their existence.

Brothers hover above . . .

as thousands of geese sit in the open fields below.

At times, the numbers are many.

At times, the numbers are few.

What matters to me is that one bird.

I feel differently than the hunter about that one bird. Yet, there is a unity which can't be denied.

The hunter is the regulator moving the flock from location to location. Managers of refuges can manipulate the flock very easily by changing the hunting pressures. If the number of geese permitted to be killed is raised, the flock numbers lower, or if the quota of birds killed is lowered, the flock increases. The hunter has a very definite role. At Horicon the hunter draws a tag in a lottery. And anyone may submit a tag whether they're a hunter or not. The whole effect has obliterated the real concept of goose hunting. Not many hunters can afford to put money into decoys, or to lease land. The goose hunting season in Wisconsin is over for many with one shot, one bird. The way it usually goes is that the hunter who wants to shoot a wild goose for Thanksgiving draws a tag; if he is lucky, he drives up to Horicon, pays a farmer living around the edge of the marsh a blind fee, ten dollars or whatever, and walks to the blind. He usually doesn't have to wait very long. The birds are concentrated, and generally unwary and eager to get to the fields to feed. They often fly right over the blind, sometimes in large numbers, so that the hunters hammer away at them. Sometimes hunters are not very good shots. Their charges scatter among the members of the flock, lodging in several bodies but not killing. The hunter may kill a bird with one shot, of course, but more likely he takes several to knock down a goose.

When he does pick up the bird, his goose hunting is over for another year; perhaps he has consumed a total of two hours. It is not at all like the old way of wild goose hunting which was a much more chancy thing, more of a pitting of man against bird, a battle of skills and knowledge, and definitely filled with more excitement. But now, at Horicon Marsh, it isn't easy to alter hunting patterns, because of the great concentration of the birds, the num-

bers of hunters, and the rights of the landowners around the marsh to rent blinds on their property. The tag and quota system has spread out the hunting, at least. It would be a frightful slaughter if there was no such system; thousands of birds could be killed in a single day. But the tag system at Horicon has definitely made the birds less cautious.

Now the flock hardly seems to even waver from a straight flight line as they head for the cornfields. The birds don't fly very high or very widely separated. Perhaps they have become fatalistic about the goose hunter, as though they know he is down there and that it is inevitable that some birds will get shot. It seems to the onlooker almost like a suicide flight. It is a little like a carnival of death: there are all sorts of hunters mixed up with goose watchers, antihunters, and everybody is there at the same time. People stand around using field glasses, observing the geese, while shotguns are popping from the blinds.

But the goose hunter is necessary, for if hunting were eliminated, the agricultural fields in a lot wider area around the marsh would be despoiled by the flock, and the goose population would explode.

A hunter's ability to kill varies with the kind of load he is using, the gun, the shot, and of course, his skill. In a concentration of birds, his skill becomes the least factor — and sixty or seventy yards is a long shot for a kill. The hunter is often misled to firing from too great distance, for the Canada goose is a large bird and looks closer to the hunter than he really is. This is why so many birds are wounded.

Whether the average hunter, but not so much the experienced hunter who may have a deep regard for the birds, ever thinks about the damage he inflicts with random or chance or foolish shots, nobody can say.

When Joe was a kid there just wasn't any goose hunting on the Horicon Marsh. If somebody in those days shot a goose, it was a big event and talked about in the taverns, and the local hunter became a momentary celebrity. Duck hunting was excellent — really good some years — but now a goose-hunting business had developed and had grown into a real part of the fall economy of the marsh area. It had sprung up as the goose flock increased in size and the hunting regulations became more stabilized.

These clubs, devoted exclusively to goose shooting, were mostly open to the general public. Anybody who had a goose permit, and who could pay the blind fee of about ten dollars per man per day, could hunt. If the hunter didn't get a goose, then he was allowed by the club to return until he did get one. For the most part, the hunters didn't return because nearly everybody who hunted at one of the clubs easily got a goose.

Some of the larger clubs had a building, perhaps a big barn, where the hunters could bring their families. The family could sit inside where it was warm, and from the barn they could watch the geese out the windows and might even be able to see where their husband or father was hunting and cheer when he brought down his wild goose. There was always hot coffee and doughnuts at the barn, free, and when the hunters were ready to go out into the field, the club managers would take them to the blinds in a pickup and get them set. If the hunters told the club people what time they wanted to come in, then they would be hauled from the blind to the barn again. Not all the hunters asked, or even liked,

to be hauled out to the locations; but the ones who were elderly, or who had infirmities of some kind, were gladly taken in a vehicle. Most of the blinds were easily seen from the office, and if the club managers saw that the hunter got his goose, they came for him.

The number of blinds varied with the size of the club farm, of course, but twenty blinds was a fairly large operation. Some of the clubs formerly had a lot more blinds, but it was hard to handle a hundred, say, and to keep track of them. The effort was concentrated. There were usually about eighteen days in the goose hunting season around the Horicon Marsh, and the middle weekend seemed always to be the big one. Sometimes a club with about twenty blinds would have more than three hundred hunters. The hunters rented a blind for the whole day. In theory, they could stay in the blind until closing for ten dollars if they wanted to, but hardly any of them did. The law allowed only one goose, and when it was shot, the hunters came back to the barn. When they returned they were asked by the club managers to permit them to rent the blind again, and the hunters always said yes, for there were a large number of people waiting. The club charged again for the same blind and might rent it several times more. On the trip out to get the hunters in the blinds, the club took two other hunters in the truck with them so that the new ones would be right there to begin. During weekdays the blinds did a brisk business, but it was on weekends that they were really kept hot.

The Wisconsin law required the operators to provide twenty acres for each blind. If a farmer owned a one-hundred acre farm, he could put five blinds on it. The blinds had to be at least a hundred yards away from a line fence, and on the other side of the fence, a competing farmer had to build his blinds a hundred yards back. The blinds then were at least two hundred yards apart. Part of the reason was safety, because some hunters weren't too careful where and how they shot; but a part of it was sheer diplomacy. For if two hunters fairly close together shot at the same bird at about the same time there could be bitter conflict over whose bird it was. Joe had seen hunters, before the regulations, come steaming out of the blinds to wrangle over a dead bird. Sometimes he had seen serious fights.

The hunters liked the spacing out of the blinds, and the farmers appreciated it, too, because they escaped having to settle arguments. Among more than a thousand hunters who used the blinds in some operations, there were now no fights or squabbles over downed birds.

Most of the blinds around the Horicon Marsh were made of wood. They weren't dug in. There were some old pits in the area, but the blinds used by the day hunters were camouflaged with grass, or cornstalks, and served very well. The blind boxes were about three and a half feet wide by six feet long — big enough to handle two men. There were benches inside, so the hunters might sit while waiting for the geese. The blinds that sat on top of the ground were apparently as effective as ones dug into the earth. Because of the huge goose flock, a hunter could very probably stand right out in the open, not use a blind, and still be successful, but that wasn't legal. The hunters had to use the blinds.

Often, on the way out to the blinds, the club men who drove the truck had to be careful not to run over geese. They were so tame and so eager to eat in the buckwheat or cornfields. Ten miles an hour was really too fast to drive, for the geese separated in front of the truck and leisurely wandered away. Often they wouldn't fly up at all.

Most of the hunters who used the club blinds were from out of the area. Almost no local people used them, probably because they had no way of making any comparisons, or any previous experience with goose hunting; the hunters who came thought blind hunting at Horicon was pretty good sport. Most of the blind hunters were from the Wisconsin or Illinois cities, and lots of them had never before shot a goose. The hunters combined a goose hunting expedition with a lot of socializing.

Most of the local people, the local hunters, and all the old-timers who had done goose and duck hunting when it was much more challenging, thought of the club operations as being like "shooting geese in a barrel." The geese were so hungry, so used to people, that the club operators had no hesitation in guaranteeing each paying hunter a goose.

In making the guarantee, the club men stipulated that the guns used had to be ten or twelve gauge, and that they used shot not smaller than number two. The hunter, to get the guarantee, had to hunt all day if necessary, from seven o'clock in the morning until closing time.

Some of the hunters brought small guns, and once in awhile bow and arrow hunters appeared at the blinds. It is legal to hunt geese from the blinds with a bow. They shot at the birds on the wing, of course, and gun hunters didn't much like the bow men. The hunting arrows, propelled by a strong bow, could travel at least one hundred yards. Fired into the air, they always came down point first. If a hunter happened to be under one he could be impaled. However, the bow hunters came out mostly during the week when the hunting pressure wasn't so great. They usually requested an open field where they had a better chance to recovering their arrows. A good bow hunter might average a goose for about sixteen arrows shot. Joe had known of some instances where a goose carried away an arrow, and he had seen one of these arrow-shot birds at the marsh, down and hardly able to move, transfixed by the arrow which had gone through the flesh at the the back of a thigh.

The people who used small guns occasionally got a goose if they waited for it to come close enough. The trouble was, the ones who hadn't hunted before shot at the first bird that came over, even if the goose was out of range. The club people often went down when they saw the senseless blasting and tried to instruct the hunters, telling them how to shoot and when to fire. A couple of hunters came to one of the clubs a couple of years back, and they had between them five boxes of shotgun shells — twenty-five shells to each box. The five boxes didn't last more than a couple of hours, then they came back to the barn for more ammunition. They bought two more boxes, and when they finally returned they each had a goose, but had fired a hundred and seventy-three times.

Once in a while a whole family arrived, and maybe each member of the family would have his own gun. The mother had packed a big lunch, and the family parked in the yard. Those of the family that had drawn a permit would go down to the blinds, and the ones left in the yard got the lunch ready. When the hunters came back with their birds, they had a merry celebrating of the successful hunt.

A lot of hunters who just arrived at the club, expecting to hunt, were ignorant about the permit system. They wanted to go right out to the blinds. But the managers told them that maybe they'd be lucky next year if they joined the lottery. Usually the hunters would have a few beers and go away, but once in a while they were nasty. Some people would do anything to shoot a goose. One of the club men told how a hunter slipped into a blind without paying the fee. They caught him, but when they looked at the goose he had shot, they saw he had tied a deer tag onto it — the law said that the hunter had to put a tag on a killed bird in the blind. The goose must not be carried to a car and tagged there. The hunter didn't get away with the deer tag. The wardens pinched him, and they never did find out whether the man knew the difference between a goose tag and a deer tag. He said he couldn't read, but the judge didn't believe him.

One thing that the club men do regret: they think that about fifty percent of the geese that are shot at the clubs aren't ever eaten at all. What happens, and this is only their guess, is that after the hunter shoots a bird he puts it in the car trunk, intending to take it into the city. He has a few beers at a club, then a few more at taverns in town, and by the time he gets the bird home, it is spoiled. There are places in the Horicon neighborhood which will pick and freeze a bird, but some of the hunters never get that far. They want only to kill a wild goose, and they will be back to do the same thing next year. The old-timers would never have wasted the geese that way. They think wasting the birds is a crime, but business is too good at the clubs to stop even the senseless killing.

The man's name was Perry Caldwell. Joe Malone was his friend, and Joe heard the story from him. Caldwell had, all his life, been fascinated by accounts of hunting adventures, and when he was a boy, had read anything he could find in the local library, or in adventures in paperbacks, about the pursuit of game. There was something in his nature, he often believed, that drove him to an appreciation of the wilderness, the hunt, the successful chase. He would like to have been born in a generation when young men went west to adventure and to hunt. A lot of his time as a lad had gone to the making of instruments of projection: slingshots made of a V fork and a handle, cut from the smaller branches of a tree, strung with rubber bands from an inner tube, and containing a leather sling cut from old shoe leather. Or he made many kinds of spears, of straight reeds growing in the lower end of the pasture, or of bamboo, old fishing poles, or carpet poles. These he learned to fling with power and accuracy. He created bows of hedge wood, and of hickory, and collected straight branches of willow or dogwood, or sometimes his folks bought him slender dowels for arrows. He had never seriously tried to kill anything with one of these weapons, though he had many times discharged the slingshot and arrows in the general direction of birds or cattle, pretending that they were elk or buffalo. Once when he was about eleven, he had made a short hunting bow, about like the ones he had read the Indians used to hunt buffalo on horseback. And he'd ridden bareback, on one of the farm work horses, to discharge homemade arrows at old Peggy, a brindle milk cow.

He wasn't bloodthirsty, exactly, it was just that he loved the idea of hunting. Like most farm boys, he acquired a small rifle when he was about twelve, and a shotgun when he was fourteen. He hunted rabbits, and many times shot quail out of coveys at the corners of Osage Orange hedgerow. His hunting adventures weren't especially thrilling, or even very interesting. The game he shot was faithfully cleaned and eaten. His folks insisted on that. But the long Saturday rambles in the woods and fields with a few companions, and a lunch to cook over a campfire, set permanently in motion his urge to be in the woods, in nature, and to carry along a gun in case there might be something to shoot.

In the country where he was raised, there were no wild ducks or any wild geese. Once in awhile the geese flew over his part of the country in their migration cycle, but he never got to shoot a duck or a goose.

When he went to college, he had little time to hunt, and he left his guns at home. He worked very hard to get an education and became an excellent student. After college, where he majored in business, he went to a job in a Wisconsin city not very far from the Horicon Marsh. He became a minor executive in a large manufacturing business, and as time went on, he became more and more able to go and come when he wished and to have time for recreation. He grew familiar with the countryside, took hikes with business companions, or with his wife. He became fascinated with the wild geese which gathered in the fall and spring at the Horicon Marsh, and in October and November, spent several Saturdays watching the birds, studying them through binoculars and making notes about their habits, their patterns of flight; and he sketched them a little, for he had taken up drawing and painting as hobbies. His sketches were rather good, though he confessed to everybody that he was just a silly amateur. He painted several pictures of the marsh settings — with reeds, water, clouds, and wild birds in flight. He loved the way geese came down onto the water and was quite successful in catching them in dramatic attitudes. He actually sold several of his paintings for very modest sums and gave others away to admiring acquaintances. He loved the way the birds wheeled, how they seemed to change the angle of their wings as they came in, how they kept their eyes always on the water, or the earth as they descended to landings. He grew to love the birds, and when he thought about his attempts at art, he considered himself a painter of wildlife. He joined several ecology organizations, and groups banded together to improve and preserve the environment. He was one of the most enthusiastic members of the local Audubon Society in his city.

The wild geese had never stirred him as a hunter until one evening, when he was at the marsh with Dick Pine, a business associate.

Dick had said, "Every time I come here I want to shoot at them."

"Do you really?" Caldwell asked. "Could you train a shotgun on 'em and keep your conscience?"

"Sure. Somebody's got to hunt. They'll all die of overpopulation."

"Honest?"

"Absolutely. Ask any scientist."

"I'd rather just study them, paint them."

"Well, you should learn to do both, hunt and paint. Most wildlife artists have been hunters, too, you know."

"Have they really?"

"Of course."

Caldwell wasn't sure this was all that true, but he accepted it. The next time he came to the marsh, the geese looked slightly different to him. He wondered how the old Indians who had once inhabited the marsh would have regarded the birds. Maybe in their time they appreciated them too, but he imagined that the Indians had chiefly thought of the birds as a source of food. He could picture the Indian hunters slipping up on a flock, concealing themselves, disguising themselves with clumps of grass or branches, finally rising, flinging off the camouflage and drawing bows to their fullest, letting the arrows go into the startled, honking birds.

The idea of the bow and arrow and the wild geese fascinated Caldwell. He remembered the thrill of making bows and arrows in his youth, and how he had cherished the notion of someday owning a real hunting bow.

He told Dick about his boyhood hunting urges one day at lunch, and Dick said, "Well, you know very well you can buy any kind of a bow you want. Maybe you'd get a kick out of bow hunting. You ought to satisfy these boyhood desires — you'd be missing something if you didn't get a bow and do a little hunting."

The idea kept moving around in Caldwell's brain, and one day he did stop in at a sporting goods store. He looked at the bows they had there, talked with the clerk about the best kind to purchase, and the best arrows to choose. The clerk asked him whether he was interested in deer hunting, and Caldwell replied that he wasn't sure what, if anything, he was going to hunt, but he'd been interested in bows since he was a kid. The clerk sold him a hunting bow and about twenty arrows, several with cutting steel tips, and few with less dangerous target points. He loved the feel of the bow and the sleek, straight arrows, recalling how he had struggled to get straight wood and to fasten chicken feathers to the shaft of homemade arrows. These store ones were quite a different matter; when he got home, he went out into the large side yard, put up a target, and began to practice.

The bow was unbelievably strong. The arrows sped swiftly and surprisingly true. He grew more and more interested and tried to get his wife to try, but the bow was too strong for her to pull, and she gave up after a try or two.

He did not give up, and over the next month bought other equipment and more arrows.

"Well, when are you going to try it on *something*?" Dick asked.

"I doubt that I'll ever shoot arrows at anything living."

"What'll you bet you don't?"

"I don't know why I should."

"Because you can't be a successful artist if you never hunt birds and animals. You can't catch the true wild spirit of game birds without hunting them. It's something in the blood that gets into the hands and the way you interpret."

"I think that sounds like hooey."

"It's not. Believe me. If you hunted, your art would get better."

Caldwell talked about Dick's theory with his wife. She said it sounded like a bunch of nonsense to her, but Caldwell wasn't sure. He recalled the thrill of hunting rabbits, squirrels, even crows, and he wondered if he could recapture the boyhood thrills if he hunted now. His wife said no, he couldn't. That was water over the dam, and he was a fool to try to ever recapture boyhood pleasures. He wasn't a boy any longer. She thought there might be a lot of older fellows trying to recapture and relive youthful pleasures; she didn't think it could be done.

Now when Caldwell went to the marsh on a Saturday, he looked at the geese in a different way. He hadn't told anyone, but he'd entered the goose hunter lottery, and the state had awarded him a permit and a tag. The law said he was entitled to kill one goose, and in his own mind, Caldwell had decided to kill a goose with an arrow. He had heard of it being done, but not so many bow hunters had done it. The old Indians had done it plenty of times. How else could they ever obtain the bird. But did they shoot geese on the wing, as the law said you had to? He didn't know, but he supposed the old Indians were so good with bow and arrow that they could easily hit a flying goose. As an experiment, he wanted to try, partly because it would be quite a thrill to draw an arrow at a goose in flight, and partly because he thought he might use the experience as the basis for some kind of a painting. Some hunter, who was fond of the bow, might pay a lot of money if he could just capture the pose, the feeling of the flight, the attitude of the bird, and catch something of the wild thrill that was in the mind of the hunter.

He scouted around the marsh area, waiting for the opening of the goose season and wondering where the best place to hunt might be. He knew you just couldn't hunt anyplace. The marsh area was a closed zone. Even bow hunters had to follow the same rules as the gun hunters. He knew that he had to hunt in a goose blind. He went finally to a large farm where goose blinds were advertised. He found the manager in the barn, and the man invited Caldwell to have a beer.

"Sure," the manager said, "we do get some bow hunters here once in a while. They have a great time. They all say the same thing: that the only real thrill in goose hunting is with bow and arrow. One guy last season got his goose on the second shot, and his wife got hers late the same day. They were really happy. They said it was the greatest thing that had ever happened to them. Both of them said that. And do you know, they said it made their marriage seem more satisfying."

"I can't see how that could be caused by shooting a goose," Caldwell said.

"Well, that's what they said. Both of 'em. Said they talked it over in the blind."

Caldwell felt a little foolish, hearing stuff like that, and it didn't interest him. It seemed very juvenile someway, but he couldn't get out of his head the idea that if he could see a goose flying above him and could draw an arrow on it, that something like an insight into art might happen — just something between him and the goose, a sense of the universal that he might transfer into a painting. And there was something else, he admitted. A feeling that the slaying of a goose, high up in the air by an arrow loosened by himself, might be self-fulfilling. He thought that the thrill of the hunt was there in him still, and the hurling of a projectile was a definite part.

He paid the club man ten dollars to reserve a place in a goose blind, and because the season wasn't open the manager took him out to see the place where he would hunt. It was a kind of box built above ground, and it had been cleverly camouflaged with cornstalks. It reminded Caldwell a little of Halloween, someway — it was sort of like a cornshock, but there was something about it that had a festival feel, a waiting feel, as though when the hunting season opened, the life of the blind would become part of a fantasy.

"This is the best place," the club manager said, "right here is where the line runs, the line that a lot of geese follow out of the marsh. You know, geese are creatures of habit, and follow the same track if they can. You'll get to shoot at geese here all right. And, too, this one is by itself. Don't want those hunting arrows falling onto hunters, do we?"

"Think my chances of getting a goose are pretty good?"

"The best."

Caldwell tried the blind for space, to see whether he could shoot from it, and found that he could. He'd have to be careful not to jostle a partner in the blind, and the manager said there would most certainly be somebody in the blind with him.

"It will probably be a gunner," he said. "I doubt that another archer will be out. If somebody does come, of course, I'll put him in here with you."

"That's all right. I don't mind who comes."

On the morning that the goose season opened at the Horicon Marsh, Caldwell got up very early so that he could be there before daybreak. His wife got up too, though he urged her not to, and fixed his breakfast. She watched as he put on his outdoor clothing: a hunting outfit with a red jacket and hat, and watched him take the bow out of its leather case, flex it, and examine the case of arrows.

"Do you expect me to cook a goose if you should hit one with that thing?" she asked.

"Either that or I'll give it away."

"I probably won't cook it. I don't think I could bear to do it. I don't see how you can even think of shooting one. If I didn't know you couldn't do it with an arrow, I'd probably throw a tantrum."

"It's aesthetic with me," Caldwell said.

"Well, I hope you keep it an aesthetic experience. You don't really strike me as a natural hunter."

"I'm an artist. I'm doing this in the cause of art."

"OK. I'll be waiting. But I don't understand why you have to shoot at geese to paint their picture."

"Well, it's kind of deep."

And it wasn't all that deep either, he knew. Really, he guessed that he simply wanted to go out and kill a wild goose. It was probably as simple as that — to feel the uplift and sensation of hunting, of loosening a bolt, of hitting, of watching, of retrieving.

"Goodbye," Caldwell said.

His wife watched him go to the car.

The drive to the hunting club wasn't very long, and Caldwell got there about an hour before the opening. Men were standing around the barn, inside and out, talking, laughing. Many had cups of coffee. The club men called out names, marked them off in a book, and the hunters were hauled in a station wagon two by two, or four by four, out into the field. The morning gave good promise of being fair; there were few clouds, and the moon, far down, seemed to throw wavy shadows as the wind moved the willows around the barn. A couple of wardens wandered among the hunters, joking, giving information. The guns of the hunters were all in cases; the men described their equipment, bragging sometimes about what a particular gun would do, what shells they used, what size shot. It was like moving soldiers out to a front-line, Caldwell thought, and he regarded his own participation with satire: *me, the longbowman, ready for the fray.* They called his name, and he walked out to the waiting station wagon.

"Gotta hurry," the driver said. "We still got quite a few to get out there."

"An awful lot of guys in there," Caldwell said, "Are they all going to hunt geese?"

"Ain't many left got a blind reserved. They're hoping they can get one after the first geese are killed. Can't shoot but one goose apiece, you know."

"Yeah, I know that."

Caldwell couldn't see the woman very clearly in the dim light. She looked slender, and he couldn't tell anything at all about her age. She had a heavy jacket on, and a leather cap.

"I guess I didn't expect to meet any lady hunters," Caldwell said.

"What's the matter. Think we're the weaker sex?"

"Oh, no."

He couldn't think of anything more to say, and the car moved out along a track at the edge of a field, then across a corner. They passed several blinds, and at a far edge, came to the blind they were to occupy.

"We figured you bow hunters ought to be together," the driver said.

"'OK. Thanks," replied Caldwell. He was very uncomfortable now and wished he didn't have to go into the blind with the woman. She took her equipment out, and she was slender, he could now see for certain. Her age? He couldn't tell, but she had a sharp, definite voice, and her statements were all positive declarations.

"It's going to be a fine morning," Caldwell said stupidly.

"Who cares? I'm here to hunt geese."

The car moved away, and the woman went to the blind. She pulled the cornstalks at the entrance aside and stepped in. "Not too much room in here."

"Any room for me?"

"Well, you paid for it didn't you? Come on in. Get settled. When the birds start coming over, we don't want to be screwing around."

She had taken off her jacket, and he could see more what she was like. She looked about thirty, short hair under her cap, a rather attractive face, he thought, very determined, and a sharpness about it, too, in the thin, small mouth. Her speech was about the same as her face: positive, clipped. He got established at an end of the blind. The box was about six or seven feet long, not very wide. The top was open, and there was a narrow bench along one side.

He took out his bow and placed arrows out where he could easily get them.

"Have you hunted very much?" Caldwell asked.

"Damned right. All over. Even out West. Mule deer. Northern Wisconsin plenty. I've shot eight deer."

"Really?"

"Three of them through the lungs. I got one through the heart."

There was a silence. Caldwell didn't know how to respond. He felt nervous and uncomfortable and wondered more and more why he had come. He couldn't respond in conversation on hunting on the woman's level. He knew that for certain. He laughed nervously.

"What did you say your name was, ma'am?"

"I didn't say. And don't call me ma'am. I'm not the housewife type exactly."

Caldwell laughed again. "I thought your name might be Diana."

"Why?"

"Well," Caldwell said, feeling very silly,

"Diana was the goddess of the hunt. From what you said —."

"Never heard of her. My name's Louise. Yours?"

"Perry."

"OK, Perry, bring over the birds."

"You hunted geese much before?"

"No. First time for geese. I want to see how good I really am. Good challenge, getting one on the wing."

It was what Caldwell had thought, too, but the way she said it turned him off. He guessed it was just target practice for her, and maybe something else, like shooting a deer through the lungs and enjoying it. Far down across the field a shotgun boomed, then another.

"I guess the season's open," Caldwell said.

They waited. It became lighter rapidly now. Far away he thought he could hear the sound of geese. Guns began to boom more often. He couldn't see anything in the sky through the top of the blind, but he sensed movement, expectancy, all around him on the earth, and a kind of urgency in the sky, as though something great and terrible was about to occur. He heard the geese then, quite loud and, he thought, quite close. His companion had strung her bow, fitted an arrow, and was searching the skies with such intentness that he almost forgot to get ready himself.

"Come on," she said, "what're you waiting for, mister? Think they'll fly into the blind so you can catch them by hand?"

He strung his bow and selected an arrow. She kept hers fitted to the string, in position, tense. A little time passed. No geese flew over them, but the guns were going all around.

"Where the hell are the birds," the woman said.

Caldwell wished desperately now that he were somewhere else. The nearness of this priestess of the hunt dismayed him. He had always thought of hunting as a pleasure, a thing to be engaged in for the joy of it, never as a humorless, stressful activity, where a bullet, or a shotgun charge or an arrow must inevitably fill psychological needs of the hunter. The game itself was of little moment, and he had the feeling that she would be equally satisfied with birds, deer, or possibly even men.

"Look," she cried suddenly.

Above them the sky was instantly filled with geese. They were quite low, and huge. Their wings stretched, necks far-out, and each body a part of the dynamism of the V of the birds. He saw, in that instant, the leader, a large bird, and he fixed his arrowpoint upon it, drawing back and back. He never knew when he released the arrow. Entranced, he saw it go, saw the flight up and up, saw its movement and direction and felt the speed of it, saw it fly well behind the bird, and forgot the arrow as the bird flew on, out of his vision. He knew that he had missed by a long, long way, and the sense of the miss did not make him unhappy. He turned to the woman, thinking that the flight of the birds might have made her relaxed, but she swore at him, violently and brutally.

"I saw you do that," she cried. "You jostled into me. Keep your own damned end of the blind. You spoiled my aim. Who the hell do you think you are?"

"Sorry," Caldwell said, amazed.

"Keep away from me. Stay there now. Stay out of my way."

The birds were coming over again. Caldwell couldn't have reached for an arrow had he wanted to. The woman fascinated him, and he watched her as she lifted the bow and drew the arrow back. The flight was a little higher than the other, but there were more birds. Her eyes were fixed and her lips moved as she sighted upward, and he saw her release the arrow, and the cry she gave was wild, primitive. Upward her arrow had transfixed a goose. He saw the final end of the action: the shaft protruding through the threshing body, the wings beating to hold the body aloft, the struggle to lift, the lessening strength, and as an obligatto to the struggle with death, the voice of the woman cursing, elated. The goose fell, faster and faster, and Caldwell, watching, wondered whether he would have observed with the same feeling of horror, if his own arrow had transfixed a bird. He saw nothing in the action that inspired any feeling of art. The bird's body crumpled in a mass of feathers and action that was without grace or beauty.

But the woman was screaming with pleasure and she kept crying, "My first arrow! First! How'd you like that, huh, huh?"

And as the goose came to earth and lay on its side with the shaft of the arrow sticking up, the woman tumbled out of the blind and rushed to it. It wasn't dead, and he could see how the bird struggled as she came to it, seized it by the neck, twisting and pulling. Caldwell thought he heard the bird give one short, agonized honk.

He took his bow and arrows and stepped out of the blind and walked away. As he departed, she called, "Hey come back! I want to see you get one. I got mine. Look!"

She held up the goose, but Caldwell didn't stop. He fled running, back toward the clubhouse.

In memory, I speak of the sunrise on the marsh.

Sunlight on the water and the birds in the morning.

Often, I see Snow Geese and Blues with the Canadas.

I watch the multitude on blue water.

I see the land and the sky merge with the birds.

The lone one thrills me with his wild power beating the water.

I sense the freedom of the lone goose in flight.

I know the birds are aware.

The hunters are a part of nature.

I would like to stand in an open field, on a small mound, with the green and gold about me.

My eyes move skyward from the blue below, to the trees, to the blue above.

It is like music in the air.

The wings beat out the rhythm on the background of heaven.

The deer are out there in the shade, in the coolness, where my senses realize change.

My questions are sometimes answered here.

I know I am alive on a winter morning; the world stands out to greet me.

The winter wood is my wonder.

Everyday draws down to great, quiet goodness.

There simply are not many old style duck and goose hunters left. A few still remain who can spin yarns of the fabulous days at the old Diana Hunting Club on Horicon Marsh, or of the great days of duck hunting on Poygan Lake, or Green Lake. And there are plenty still down south at Illinois refuge country who remember the goose hunting of the old sandbar days. But most of the great hunters and the great stories are no more.

Joe's father was a close friend of old Mieske, on whose farm the Diana club was located. At the Mieske farm, nothing remains now except a few large trees, becoming ragged, which were probably there long, long before Mieske settled even, and under which the farmhouse sat at the edge of the marsh. Of the old Diana club nothing at all remains. Joe knows the location very, very well, for in his youth he pushed some of the last hunters there into the marsh in their sharp-nosed boats, poling through the heavy vegetation. Not long ago, Joe had gone out to the location of the Diana. He hadn't been there for a long, long while, on what they once called Clubhouse Island. And in the old days it was an island, too. But when the state took over the property, they filled in the low places so that a road might be constructed. So the island is not an island any longer.

Joe recalled how many evenings he had gone with his father in their buckboard, which had a rear seat across the wagon bed, to pick up the duck hunters as they climbed down from the train from Chicago and Milwaukee. The engineer habitually stopped at the crossroad, about a mile from the club, to let hunters off and maybe to pick hunters up. There was no station at all there, but the place was widely known as the Diana Stop.

The clubhouse had been built in the 1880s of Georgia pine; certain club members, lumbermen from Oshkosh, had a great supply of the heavy Georgia timber on hand in their yards. This they gave to the club. Joe recalled well the day the state started the dismantlement of the clubhouse in the 1930s, and how strange he felt as he saw the great beams come down. It was like a whole part of his history had ended, and his family's history, and the history of the whole area — something stopped, and the wrecking of the Diana was like the beginning of something entirely new, entirely different.

The clubhouse had sat out on the very edge of the marsh, with a special ditch running right to the door, almost, and a porch where the club members could look out across the marsh, marveling often at the vast loneliness of the scene as it was then and observing the great flocks of birds: ducks, of course, hardly any geese then, and the flocks of blackbirds and swallows, and the redwings which clung to the taller cattails and dogwood.

On the knoll where the Diana stood, nothing on the surface of the earth remains to tell the story. Joe spent an entire day there, and he remembered how he had scraped around in the dirt and among the tangle of growth, for much can happen to a location in fifty years. Trees, and sizable ones, too, were growing where the porch had run across the front. Brush, so thick that it was very hard to break through, cluttered the old kitchen door location. Scraping here and there with a spade, Joe turned up many objects buried under the sod: bits of china, and once an entire dish, a handsome piece of English stoneware, many square nails, numbers of brass ends of shotgun shells, and once a whole old brass shell. The remnants he put carefully in a cardboard box and took home with him and put in his basement.

He didn't know what he'd do with them, but they were there, as reminders.

He had, that day, walked a little way out along the Burnet Ditch, one of the cross ditches into the marsh, for he remembered that at the end of it had once been the hulk of the old Horicon Lake steamboat, wrecked so many, many decades ago and left to rot. He could see nothing of the hulk and supposed the last parts of it had sunk into the mud, for he remembered the last time he had gone out to look, some of the wood could still be seen a little above the marsh surface. You had to know where.

Of the old hunters, there were only memories. Captain Ewing, tall, white bearded, in his late seventies when Joe knew him as a boy, had told how he hunted ducks in the marsh right after the Civil War. He had brought home with him a musket picked up on the Wilderness Battlefield, and the then young Captain had hunted with the musket, loading it with shot. And he had bagged hundreds of mallards. In those days there was no limit on ducks. The very first state law closing hunting was enacted in 1872, but it was rapidly repealed in 1880. The law was reinstated in 1891, but it wasn't until 1905 that spring hunting was stopped in Wisconsin.

Captain Ewing had told of the great kills of ducks, the almost senseless slaughter. Some hunters bagged from twenty-five to a hundred ducks a day, using muzzle-loading shotguns fired with percussion caps. The market hunters mounted punt guns on the skiffs and loaded the muzzles with a charge of one pound of shot to each barrel. Ducks were shot as they sat resting on the water, sometimes more than a hundred were killed in a single blast. Captain Ewing never knew exactly what became of the great numbers of ducks killed. Some were shipped away packed with ice in barrels, to distant restaurants, he supposed, but it just had to be a fact that many killed ducks were wasted, for there was no home freezing in those days.

Joe often thought how glad he was that the great flocks of Canadas had not come in those early years. Like the buffalo on the Great Plains, they would have been extinguished by the frenzy and the greed of man.

No, the hunting days would never come again. In place of the Diana club and the lolling millionaires on the front porch, now there were a thousand goose hunters in pits, blasting away at the Canadas, each hunter allowed one bird. There was something sad when Joe compared the old, free hunting life, which was wasteful at times, but not nearly so canned as the modern methods of hunting.

The trouble with hunters, Joe thought, was that the good ones had conquered themselves and learned what their real motivations to kill were. The poor ones never did learn, or had too little opportunity to learn. It was a two-headed beast and thus very, very difficult to control. If all the hunters could be good ones in the great struggle between good and evil, then the goose problem wouldn't be so great. The good ones never took advantage of the birds; the good ones never tried to kill at impossible distances. They used the proper guns of larger gauge — the little guns too often maimed and did not kill. The good ones took only what they were allowed. They might have regrets that the quota was low, but they respected the birds and their welfare far, far too much to ever break the code.

Not the bad ones. Joe remembered the many times he had seen illegal practices among the bad hunters — the killing of a goose and the concealing of the body to be retrieved later; the shifting of tags from one bird to another after the bird had been checked; the hasty plucking and cleaning of the birds in secluded places, and the carcasses concealed, even upon a hunter's person.

Each one had his own code. Things that he would or wouldn't do. The irritation and disgust with the careless hunters ran deep, as Les, an old friend and local hunter had spoken of just a few days ago, remembering certain things that had happened.

"I was huntin' in a hole up here some years back," he had said, "and there was three guys. They was just right off of me, and I tell you, they shot at them ducks high, and they don't knock any down where they can recover them. So I says, 'How many ducks you guys got?' I says, 'I bet you shot down ten and you didn't get back a one. You got a limit of five each, and how many are you going to knock down to get those fifteen ducks you are allowed? I guess you'd have to destroy about a hundred ducks. You guys are wasteful. Guys like you shouldn't even be on the marsh.'

"I get madder'n hell. I cuss 'em out. I get so darn disgusted I can't hold it. I was always taught, if there's somebody huntin' in that one pothole, you go and look for a different hole. My dad always believed in the rule that you should always be at least a good gun and a half away from the next hunter. There was a guy from the Conservation Department several years ago, come up here and says to me, take me huntin' with you. So I took him up by the Four Mile Pond where there is a small hole. We went in there early in the morning, and all of a sudden I see three boats. It is then a little after daybreak. They didn't have decoys, but they come in and put themselves right around *our* decoys. So I says to them, if a duck comes over what way are you gonna shoot? And then here comes a teal, low. Bang! Bang! Bang! Right towards us. So I says to those guys, you're poor sportsmen. Where's your decoys?"

"We don't need no decoys," they says.

"Well, I says, you don't need no decoys because you're usin' *my* decoys.

"When I come home from the war, it was about 1946, I went with a couple of friends up to the north end of the marsh. Out by the refuge, and the guys was standin' elbow to elbow along there, and when a guy knocked a goose down, the first guy to get to it, it was his, no matter if he shot it or not. Ole Schmidt, he knocked one down, and he run into the willows to get his goose. He had it in his hand, and another guy come runnin' up and grabs it out of Ole's hand. These two guys started fightin', still holding onto their guns. I yells, 'Ole, let the so and so have it. A goose ain't worth gettin' killed over.' "

"Well, I hope he croaks when he eats it." says Ole, and he lets go of the goose.

"That's the last time I ever went up there. Now they got the hunting better organized. Them clubs, they do a pretty good job, if you like that kind of hunting in a blind with tame geese flying right on top of you.

"The hunter today is mostly a wasteful man. My dad, he taught me to leave the ducks come over the hole. When the duck is coming down with his legs ready to land, then that's the time to shoot."

There was that time in 1966, when the federal and the state men had joined to try and disperse the goose flock from the marsh. If they could do it, get the birds to seek other refuges, then the flock could be decreased in size to its advantage. Joe and others were afraid that if the hazing went vigorously it would drive the birds out of the refuge. But the arguments weren't convincing, and the plan went ahead anyway. State and federal government were to cooperate in driving the geese away.

The plans had all been made and the hazing of the birds was about to start when the Conservation Department in Madison began to feel the public pressure. An official of the department, not Gray, who had retired by that time, but who might have done the same, let it be known that the state would arrest federal men who participated in the bird hazing. Wardens were actually sent to the federal headquarters to warn the workers there. And the cooperative program was cancelled. The federal men, however, conducted very active hazing on the federal land. A lawsuit was started to prevent the hazing. The federal workers continued in the week just prior to the hunting season with a helicopter, two fixed wing aircraft, two airboats, two marsh vehicles, six conventional boats, fifteen floating platforms mounted with crop protection exploders, sixteen land-based exploders, and lots of firecrackers.

The Horicon Marsh then, Joe had thought, reminded him of World War II, with guns going all day, aircraft buzzing, and screaming, frightened geese flying in every direction. The marsh men watched the hazing and hoped for success, for they all realized that the goose flock was too large. But they hated the thought of what would happen when the hunting season started. The hazing was stopped twenty-four hours before the opening of the season, but the damage had been done as far as the birds were concerned. They came back to roost in the marsh at night, but now, frightened to stay, they flew wildly and carelessly out of it in the morning.

Again, Joe thought, it was like a war. The hunters stood elbow to elbow, and as the birds came over, they fired and fired throughout a seven county area. The kill was terrible. The season closed in two and a half days. Throughout the whole state the kill was thirty-one thousand birds, more than twice the desired number.

And again, as Joe and the rest of the marsh men saw, there was a great waste of birds. Hundreds were wounded and many were shot that were never picked or cleaned.

But so it went. And in the battle to save the geese, would the refuge men end by destroying the birds? The old-timers said, yes, they would. The birds would get diseased and die. But Joe didn't really believe that. It was a possibility, of course. But the biologists would find a way to prevent that, surely.

There were many, many ways to evade the law. Joe had grown through the years to hate the bad hunters. He had known himself the joys of the hunt, the anticipation which had always partly been the thrill of being out, being with nature, walking, searching, seeing the start of the bird or the animal, himself against it, and against himself. The wildness was there in him, he knew, and perhaps that was why he also felt a deep kinship for the wild things — a kinship that grew as he grew in feeling and understanding; and finally, as of now, as of his old age, as of his retirement, as of his wisdom, a thing so deep he could not describe the feeling. He knew it as love for the birds, and the desire to kill had entirely disappeared.

If, he thought, all of those who hunt, the good and the bad, could have lived my life, could have seen the wild things come back on this marsh, could have seen the water return, could have seen the programs of reclaimation, of nurturing the land and the wildlife. If they could have been with him on that early morning long, long ago, when he was just home from World War II, and he had gotten up early to go out alone, as of now, for the need, the urge for solitude was so, so strong. And he had left Mary sleeping in their bed, the same one they still used, and he had walked out, far along the dryer grounds. He had come up quietly and unknowing, for he had anticipated nothing, and suddenly the birds were there, all around him, and with a great, sudden noise and clapping of wings and loud honking, the flight arose out of the cornfield. He had been stunned, for never before had he seen any large number of Canada geese in the marsh. They had simply not been there during his early life, and he could not understand why they were there now. But they were there rising, great wings beating so thick and close together he could hardly distinguish one bird from another. He was close to them, really among them, and for an instant they were all around him and above him, and in an instant they were gone.

He had believed that there must be several hundred — perhaps a thousand in the flock; and he was unbelieving. Yet he had seen the wonder, the miracle it was to him. He did not know what had caused the great flock to come so suddenly to the marsh; but poetically he was moved in a way he had never been moved before. The war years had been long and terrible. He had been in Europe, in some of the worst of it, and he had believed that he would never again see beauty, feel the poetry of wild movement, be alone to appreciate, to drink in, to be, and to become.

Yet in an instant he had been able to do this. Probably it was then that the love of the birds began. If he had to put a finger on the moment in time, that was it. And it had apparently been the first real enlargement of the goose flock which from that time came again, and again in vaster numbers to the marsh, larger and larger, until, as of the present, the flock was two hundred thousand, maybe more. It had not been easy to lure them. From their first attempts with a couple of hundred goslings, it had been hard work.

The research scientists at the state headquarters said that most likely it was just that a few birds stopped, found feed, returned, and others came. Little by little, the flock began to build up; but Joe was never really satisfied with this explanation. The arrival of the Canada geese seemed a miracle, and he personally attributed it to some force, some factor that was somehow beyond research. And, in fact, the geese were responsible for a part of his restlessness, for his excitement, and the feeling of always wanting to be doing something he believed had always been the eagerness and liking he felt for his job. He simply couldn't wait to get the sun up so that he could begin what had always been to him, a fascinating occupation.

The female goose had been wounded about a month before, early on a Thursday morning. She wouldn't have known that it was Thursday, but the man who shot her knew it well. Thursday was his day off work, and he'd driven out to the hunting grounds with a pal, George Enfield. Neither of them knew very much about hunting geese. George had shot a few, he said, several years ago, and hadn't forgotten how much fun he'd had. He told about a big poker game they had that night before he went hunting; he'd won a few dollars, had drunk some really good whiskey. His stories of the hunting trip had persuaded Harry to go. Harry had had to borrow a gun, a twenty-gauge double, and the shells he'd purchased were ordinary twenties, not magnum. The shot was size six; the outfit wasn't particularly good for geese. Harry didn't know that, and George didn't have enough knowledge to help very much.

They left on Wednesday night after work. They both worked at the same place, a small factory on the edge of a small city a hundred miles from the Horicon Marsh. They drove over to Horicon together, rented a double room at a small, inexpensive motel, and the next morning early, drove out to the goose club to occupy the goose pit they had reserved. Both of them had joined the goose lottery, and both had drawn tags.

Harry said he felt very excited, and he looked it. His hands shook when he took the borrowed shotgun out of the case; and he spoke in a nervous, tense way when he loaded the gun and remarked how sleek and beautiful it looked.

The pit was a small one at the side of a cornfield. The two men hunched down, cradling their weapons, and the farmer who owned the farm and rented the pits told them that the geese would come over, he was sure, a little after dawn.

The sun was just coming up when they heard the honking. Down and across the field a gun exploded, then another. George and Harry peered out carefully, and suddenly saw the five geese. George swung around, jostling Harry and Harry was so excited he couldn't speak; he jerked his shotgun up, took a general aim at the birds and pulled the trigger. He shot the left barrel first, then the right one. He had no idea that he had hit anything; but suddenly George, who hadn't fired because Harry had hogged the space, cried, "Look, one's comin' down."

One of the geese had fallen behind the others and was circling slowly, flying with great difficulty. It was indeed coming down, but not near them, and finally they saw the bird flutter to earth several hundred yards away and beyond the edge of the preserve, back into the refuge. Harry started to crawl out of the pit. He wanted to go and retrieve the goose, but George pulled him back.

"We can't go over there. They're safe when they are in the refuge. Don't worry. We'll get a chance at plenty more."

The goose, that morning, had been wounded in the breast, in the wing, and one leg. Harry, with no skill at all and with light shot, had reached her quite by chance. She was a little too high to be killed anyway, but the shot had inflicted painful and crippling damage. One wing had stiffened and had become useless for flight. The pain in her breast was constant and sharp at first, then, with days, it began to diminish. She walked, but painfully, for there were several shot lodged against the bones in her right leg. Since she had been hurt, she'd ranged along the edge of the ditch, had gone to the water often, and was able to swim. Food was a problem, since she found it difficult to forage, and she had come down in an area where most of the corn had long ago been gleaned by the thousands of geese in the area. She was quite alone. She saw geese fly over constantly and heard shooting for several days; then the season ended, and there were no more shots. She survived on the few seeds of the weeds and grasses, and gleaned some food out of the ditch. She spent all day in the water, or on the bank.

At times she was sure she heard her mate calling her. She thought she saw him fly over her location several times, but when the migration south began, the birds left the marsh, and her mate, if it was he, if he'd escaped the hunters, must have gone too.

One night the cold came suddenly and snow fell. She huddled against the bank edge, calling softly in distress, for now she could hardly drag herself out of the water. Hunger, pain, and the open wounds, sapped her strength. In the night she thought she heard the fox. There were many near, always hunting for the hurt birds, and she knew that her time would come. Then the fox would leap upon her, bite quickly into her neck, and that would be the end of it.

It was early the next morning when she heard the sounds. She could not move, for the cold had stiffened her injured leg and her whole side was full of pain. She cowered against the bank, and then as she saw the shadow, tried to shove out into the water. But something had her. She was held firmly. She screamed for her mate and tried to slap the thing which held her with her wings. Only one wing moved, and that one feebly.

Then the voice spoke. It said, "Now, now, I've got you. Don't struggle, poor thing."

The man lifted her and bore her carefully to the cage that had a carrying handle. She was transported, she knew not where, over rough land, through snowy fields, beside tall marsh grasses. And at length to the pen.

There were many other geese there. Cripples, like herself. She was borne to the gate, and the man lifted her out of the cage. She was placed carefully on the ground. Painfully, she moved toward the other geese.

"How many this week, Joe?"

"Maybe fifteen, I dunno."

"Well, the Lord'll remember you."

"I dunno," Joe said. "I can't just let them die. If a fox got them fast, that'd be all right, I guess. It's nature's way. But just dying, out there, no fault of theirs — it's cruel. I been watchin' this one for a week now. She might not make it. But with enough food, she might."

"You never can tell."

Joe Malone had sojourned several times in southern Illinois at the refuges, and at Cairo. He took Mary once, and they visited a veterinarian at Du Quoin, formerly a friend from the Horicon area, who knew and related the violent history of the country. Later Joe thought that there was nothing in the memory of any living Canada goose that would make it recall the bloody events that transpired in Williamson County, Illinois, on the morning of June 22, 1922. Many generations of geese have come and gone since then; and in any event, the geese were long gone on their northward migration before the terrible events took place. But upon their southward flight in October, had they been able to see and to comprehend, they would have known the bitterness and hate that was left in the wake of the Williamson County massacre.

Who knows how the lives of the people of southern Illinois were changed and altered by those happenings; or, for that matter, how the eventual fate of the geese was affected. More than seventeen thousand acres of Williamson County, Illinois, is now the Crab Orchard National Wildlife Refuge. The main seat of the troubles was at Herrin, only a couple of miles north of the refuge.

The people at Herrin, these days, seem to be devoted to wildlife, to hunting and to fishing, and are very, very proud of their wonderful Crab Orchard Lake where bass fishing is, maybe, the best anywhere in the world.

In the taverns at Herrin, talk is almost always about hunting and fishing — the events of the mine troubles, and the bitter trials, the murders, are not much mentioned now except casually.

What happened in 1922 was that the Southern Illinois Coal Company had opened a strip mine between Herrin and Marion in Williamson County. In April, the United Mine Workers went on strike; but the owner of the Southern Illinois Coal Company decided to continue operations despite warnings that the local workers would not tolerate it. They imported strikebreakers from Chicago, mainly, and from that moment the big troubles began. Mobs formed, and wild talk of violence circulated. Peacemakers tried their best; the local sheriff was appealed to time after time. He would not act. The attempts to call out the National Guard were thwarted by poor communications and by an indecisive governor. A truce between the union miners and the strikebreaking workers at the mine was tried. It didn't turn out as hoped. By the early morning hours of June 22 it was too late. Violent action was inevitable. The strikebreakers were barricaded behind railroad ties and crouched under railroad coal cars. They were armed, but so were the angry men who surrounded them. Firing began. At last the besieged men offered to surrender. They were marched toward the town of Herrin, and enroute nineteen were murdered.

The affair attracted great attention nationally. Demands for justice were shouted. Trials were held, but no convictions were obtained.

Driving through the Crab Orchard refuge in Williamson County today the beauty, the wild, lonely roads, the wild blue lake, the serene sight of thousands of Canada geese feeding and bathing — all these things seem out of step with violence and human hatred.

Perhaps the geese and what they have come to mean to the area in income have had a great deal to do with the disappearance of violence, human feuds, killing. Or perhaps the opportunity to hunt geese has sapped the men of the area of their potential violence.

On the far eastern edge of Crab Orchard refuge is the old city of Marion, Illinois. Marion is the county seat of Williamson County and was the scene of many court trials during the hard days of vendetta and prohibition. Before the Civil War, it was the home of John A. Logan and Robert G. Ingersoll. Both noted men were admitted to the bar at Marion. Both men became colonels of regiments which they organized. Both men were among the greatest public speakers America has produced. Logan's oratory was important in winning southern Illinois for the Union cause. Robert Ingersoll was probably as widely known in his day as any speaker in the United States. His views were revolutionary for his time, liberal, and impatient with conventional moral values and puritan attitudes. Had Robert Ingersoll been alive when the great Canada goose issue became so vital to southern Illinois, he would probably have been at the forefront of conservationists and wildlife refuge makers.

The great vendettas and blood feuds that tore the country in post-Civil War times and resulted in the killing of a number of persons, are no more. In place of the notoriety of the feuding families, the country is now famous for geese and more geese. Folks come to fish, too, and to hunt quail and other birds, but it is the Canada geese that are the big news now, and local folks love the birds and do what they can to protect them.

The Crab Orchard National Wildlife Refuge was established in 1947. It is about fifty miles north of Horseshoe Lake, near Cairo; the large acreage of cropland furnishes food for many thousands of the geese and takes some pressure off of Horsehoe Lake. The operation has been a success.

The Union County refuge, further south, was acquired by the Illinois Conservation Department in the late 1940s. When it became apparent that the goose flock was declining, some additional refuges became vital. By 1964, the Union County refuge developed a wintering goose population of fifty thousand. As its

part of the flock which numbers in all of the southern Illinois refuges about three hundred thousand, Union County now has about eighty-five thousand birds. Union county refuge contains 6,202 acres in the bottomlands of the Mississippi River. Shallow sloughs meander through the area, and there are two lakes, Grassy Lake and Lyerla Lake. The geese at the Union County refuge do not hesitate to come right up to the refuge headquarters. They feel safe there and very secure in the attitudes of the refuge managers, who make no secret of their deep fondness for the birds. At the south end of the Union County refuge, there is a public hunting grounds. Hunting is on a permit-only basis, with permits issued at Springfield upon application. The daily fee is five dollars. Fifty blinds are located on the grounds, which can accommodate one hundred hunters each day. A drawing is held each morning during the hunting season to allocate the blinds.

Southern Illinois, the home of the wintering goose, is an attractive and even lush and hilly country. It has always been a country of game; in the earliest days it was inhabited by large herds of buffalo. They had gone by the nineteenth century; but there were elk, deer, bear, wolves, foxes, raccoon, opossums, and squirrels. The news of the large amount of wild animals and birds caused many of the settlers to become essentially hunters and fishermen instead of farmers. There were wild turkey in great abundance, rabbits, quail, and prairie chicken. And in the rivers and lakes were innumerable bass, pickerel, muskellunge, catfish, perch, eels, suckers, bluegill. And there were the prairies: level ground, covered with beard grass and tall flowers: oxeye, sunflowers, iron weed, goldenrod, aster, milkweed, lilies, wild roses, purple cornflowers, marigolds, and bluebells. The settlers came with the inevitable plow, of course, and the prairies did not long remain unbroken. There were orchards, too; peaches did very, very well, and so did apples.

When visitors came, they remarked about the huge magnolias that were waxy, then suddenly brown and shrivelled, the tulip tree, azalea, dogwood, and horsechestnut.

There were thickets of crabapple and red-haw. The wild plum bloomed in misty white in the spring. Red, black, and white oaks covered the clay hills; sassafras trees, persimmons with puckery, sweet fruit. The American red bud, prickly ash, honey locust, Ohio buckeye, and Kentucky coffee tree added tone and flavor.

In the old days, the taller trees were surrounded by shrubs, the hop tree, honey bush, spice bush, buttonbush — and over these often grew vines: grapes, passionflower, moonseed. It was then a wild and beautiful and primitive country.

Now, of course, things have changed, though the land has a unique character and a feeling often of solitude. The geese which are in the skies and in the fields contribute to a feeling of wildness and help the human imagination to cast the land into visions of the past.

Before the white men came to southern Illinois, there were the Indians. When the French explorers came first into the Mississippi Valley, they found a confederacy of five tribes inhabiting the country which was named after them, the Illinois. During the eighteenth century, these tribes were nearly annihilated by the surrounding peoples. By 1818, the Cahokia, the Michigamea, and the Tamaroa had disappeared as distinct tribes. The Kaskaskia, weakened, lingered in a reservation of three hundred and fifty acres left them near the town of Kaskaskia. The remnants of the Peroia still lived near their former habitat near the Illinois River. The Kickapoo were scattered from the headwaters of the Kaskaskia River to the Illinois. Further north were the Sacs and Fox, located near the mouth of the Rock River. The legends and names of these peoples still give atmosphere to the State of Illinois. In the 1830s, the remaining warriors of the Kaskaskia and Peroia tribes decided to emigrate to the southwest; an Indian leader in southern Illinois was Du Quoin, who possessed and at times wore, a medal presented to him by George Washington when Du Quoin visited at Philadelphia.

The first white men in southern Illinois were French. In 1681, La Salle and a party of fifty-four Indians and Frenchmen travelled down the Illinois River, reached the Missis-

sippi, and halted at the great village of the Tamaroa Indians. The place was named Cahokia. From there the party went on down the river, reached its mouth, and took possession of the river and the territory it drained into. Subsequent small groups of Frechmen drifted down the river to Cahokia and on to the mouth of the Kaskaskia River, where they settled and named the place Kaskaskia. Cahokia and Kaskaskia became the first permanent settlements in Illinois.

Settlers came thick and fast after the War of 1812. Steamboats began to navigate the Ohio River, main artery to the west, and brought hundreds. Many hundreds also floated down the river on their own in flatboats, keelboats, and rafts. Although there were difficulties with the Indians who remained in the country, the land about the mouth of the Ohio and northward began to fill up. Some of the place names found in southern Illinois show that the settlers had found a promised land. They went to the Bible for many: Eden, Joppa, Lebanon, and Shiloh. They were fond of names from the Nile Valley: the whole section was called "Egypt." They established Cairo, Thebes, and Karnak. Founders of Independence, Liberty, and Equality summed up the pioneer spirit. Many of these settlers were from older, long-settled parts of America. They were restless, independent, strong willed. They were clever craftsmen: blacksmiths, cabinetmakers, coopers. Even today some of these crafts persist.

Far, far past generations of Canada geese have seen all of this happen. The ancestors of some of the birds that winter at Horseshoe Island, at Crab Orchard or Union County, must have roosted on the sandbars when the old Indians were present; and no doubt, the Indians often feasted upon wild goose. When La Salle and his party went downriver, they probably startled Canada geese on the sandbars, and perhaps these early explorers had the same sensations of awe and breathless excitement that modern bird lovers feel when they watch the tremendous flights of wild geese.

The geese are leaving Horicon Marsh for their wintering ground. Joe watches them go on a gray day in late November. Last night it turned very cold, and he knew that very likely they would go today. He has gone out into the marsh to see the early ones depart. They have been very restless. Some small family groups have wandered nervously, and a circular movement has gone on within the larger collection of the birds standing or walking around on the once green field. Above there are skittish groups circling, some getting higher and higher, and then they begin to leave. The high ones turn, point southward, and will not return. Others move, rise, wheel, circle, and mount higher and higher. They follow the first flight. And so, on and on. More and more geese rise. Now the field is almost empty. Joe turns toward his car. He is overcome by a deep sadness. It has happened again. It will happen again and again.

"And if I am only here to see it . . ."

At the refuges in southern Illinois, at Union County and Crab Orchard and Horseshoe Lake, there have been geese arriving for sometime. There seem to always be geese there, the wounded ones from the previous season may have made it through the season past. Some have flown directly down from the northland nesting grounds. But the big influx, the vast flock, the big migration, has not arrived. The men are ready.

Earlier this morning the young manager of the Union County refuge has had a telephone call from his friend, the biologist at Horicon Marsh.

"I think this is it," the biologist says. "Last night it turned very cold up here and the wind is up. I believe they will go today."

He has been calling down to his friend for several years with the news of the flock's departure. And the young manager at the refuge can hardly wait for the birds to arrive. There are several of the birds he can easily recognize; he hopes fervently that he will see them, that they will have escaped the fall hunt at Horicon Marsh, for he, like Joe, has the feel of the wild things in his blood, and they furnish poetry to his soul.

Horseshoe Lake refuge, north of Cairo, was established in 1927 when the Illinois Department of Conservation made an initial purchase of about thirty-five hundred acres which included Horseshoe Lake, an ancient oxbow of the Mississippi River, and the island it surrounds. At that time, the area was operated as a duck marsh, and only an occasional Canada goose was shot there during the hunting season.

Following the purchase, Horseshoe was established as a game refuge, and the Illinois Department of Conservation began a development program aimed at attracting Canada geese. The program was most successful from this standpoint. The supply of food and the safety afforded by the refuge soon attracted Canada geese from the sandbars of the Mississippi River, which had been their ancestral wintering grounds. Later, the Mississippi River became less attractive because development of the nine-foot channel for navigation destroyed many of the large sandbars which formerly served as wintering grounds for these geese. Increased hunting pressure, the absence of annual June floods which had previously scoured the sandbars, and a change in harvesting practices for corn and soybeans — all contributed in making the Mississippi from Saint Louis, Missouri, south to the Mississippi River delta, less attractive to Canada geese.

At Horseshoe Lake Park, Bill Collins, in his small office at the deserted public campgrounds, senses something and steps outside. From high and faraway, he hears the honking; he looks across the water toward the island, the land between the arms of the horseshoe, and in the tall, dead tree he sees the two eagles. Perhaps they too have heard the geese and are waiting. The cypress trees on either side of the refuge road are standing deep in water. On their trunks, four feet higher than the present water level, is the mark of very high water, going back to the swirling flood of 1973. The day is gray, silent. The trees are ghostly, bare. The state sign beside the road says that the road will be closed on October 15 until the end of the migratory bird season. When the birds come back, the refuge is solely for them.

In Cairo, the small, old city, the city of the meeting of the Ohio and the Mississippi rivers, and of long traditions of geese and goose hunting, Bob Lansden, a friend of Joe's sits in a back room of the Security Bank and tells of geese and goose hunting. Bob is tall, neatly dressed in a gray flannel suit, a patrician; sixty-five years old, his family is long-standing in Cairo country.

"We have heard the flock referred to," said Bob, "as the Mississippi Flyway geese, but apparently there are darned few geese that go further south from here. The report I heard many years ago was that the folks in Louisiana shot off their geese down there. It's always been my understanding that geese can absolutely be exterminated by man. You could lose all the ducks in North America without firing a shot because of botulism, fires, farming and disease, but the geese go to areas for breeding which are free of all that sort of stuff; up there in the James Bay area, they breed up there, and there's no way in God's world a man can bother them too much. But we saw what happened here. There was an overkill here in the late thirties and forties, and although the National Fish and Wildlife Service did rig a few figures to make it seem a

lot worse than it was, the flock did get down to around fifty-eight thousand birds. They said the figure was twenty-six thousand, or something like that, but we conducted some aerial surveys and found there were about twice that many.

"Now, however, there's plenty of geese down here, and of course that was the starting of the dispersal program and the building of the Satellite refuges, at Puxico, Missouri and Kentucky Woodlands, that little place up there at the mouth of the Wabash. Crab Orchard got developed, and the really successful one for geese, of course, is Union County. So the birds are here, but I can remember in the old days, every damn goose on the Mississippi Flyway came through Horseshoe Lake. And there isn't any doubt that the creation of the preserve at Horseshoe Lake took 'em off the sandbars and brought 'em into the preserve. There isn't any doubt about that.

"That was sandbar hunting in the old days. And it extended largely down to what we call the 'Dogtooth Bend' area, and along the western edge of Alexander County, and roughly, you might say, from two or three miles south of Thebes, all the way down the western edge of Alexander County. Well, in the old days, the birds were on the sandbars. There is a daily migration of the flock from the preserve to the sandbars, because they must have river sand to lubricate their crops. Sand is essential to the digestive system of a goose. It will keep them from being crop bound.

"Well, we learn the hard way sometimes, everybody does, even the various departments of the federal government, too. We learn the hard way about how to feed these birds when they need feed, or how you protect 'em from their own ravenous appetites. We had one year serious crop binding in geese because it was so dry. They would eat soybeans and the beans would swell in their crops. They'd choke to death. They'd eat grass that was too dry. They've since learned, don't ever feed soybeans to geese. They've since learned to feed 'em corn, let 'em take it off the shell. And another thing, if you're interested in a real vital statistic, any portion of an ear of corn that's within forty-two inches of the ground, the goose will get it all without ever taking it off the stalk. He will take the corn right out from inside the husk, and you'll open it up and there isn't a thing inside there but a cob. They're clever that way.

"We used to operate the biggest hunting club on Horseshoe Lake. We had a mile and a half along the west bank. Our club and the one next to it, the so-called Wicker Club, killed sixty percent of all the geese in Alexander County. I kept the figures myself in the 1939, 1940, and 1941 seasons. We were averaging two and a half geese per man per day. We had several days when the limit was four, with thirty hunters, and they killed a hundred and twenty geese. The opening day of the season in 1939, the limit was four, fifty-four hunters killed two hundred and sixteen geese. Then they started the arrangement of changing the limits. They had it three geese in any seven consecutive days — three in one day, and then you couldn't shoot for a week. Then they got it down to two, and they've never very much changed it since. They've played around with daily possession, and that sort of stuff.

"Do you know my friend Harold Hanson, at the Illinois National History Survey? Well, Hanson knows more about this flock of geese that flies up and down the Mississippi Flyway than any other living person. He has scientifically studied that flock of geese continually since before World War II. He knows more about these birds than anything else. He's got the most marvelous collection of goose carcasses, wings, heads, feet. He had determined that there is an enormous number of subspecies in Branta canadensis, and that the subspecies are due to environmental reasons: differences in the habitat where they nest. He has this project. You know, he gets the birds, and then he burns the feathers, and then has the feathers chemically analyzed by the Metalurgical Institute at the University of Illinois. After he gets the report on the metal content in the feathers, he can tell you where that bird nested. It's as colorful as this: he once came up with some very high copper content in the feathers. It was so high that he wrote to the major copper companies in Canada and asked whether they knew that there were immense copper deposits up in the far north where the geese nested. They said 'Yes they knew about them, but they didn't know how to get at 'em.'

"But Hanson's one real thing that he did, and he did it rather easily, was the giant Canada Goose, the Maxima — when he was reading in the books that they were thought to be extinct, and starting with his visit to the municipal reservoir in Rochester, Minnesota, and to the state Capitol grounds in Pierre, South Dakota, Denver, and other places, he reached the conclusion that there were some forty-five to sixty thousand Maxima birds still floatin' around. Now they don't come down here. Normally those birds don't come down this far. Their migratory pattern will bring them to northern Illinois, and to the lake district of northern Illinois, where it's a little colder in the winter and, of course, being a big bird, they are strong enough to handle it. But Hanson has instances in his book of eighty-four inch wingspreads — and twenty-two and twenty-four pound birds.

"Well, there have been a few shot down here, but a very few. One of my friends who ran a saloon, he got one one day that weighed seventeen or eighteen pounds. But the Maxima is a separate subspecies — there isn't any doubt; the profile of their heads — they have a very pronounced promontory that makes their silhouette entirely different from an ordinary Canada goose.

"There's a little story. You know, how to tell the sex of a goose is some problem. During World War II, Hanson devised a way of doing it, and after the war he found that a Japanese scientist had come up with exactly the same method. I don't know much about it, but I guess that up at Horicon Marsh they let the gander figure it out for himself.

"Well, geese are monogamous. Awhile back, the government was always talking about broken pairs — you know, we shoot one mate and not the other. Our experience was, and we saw it day after day, after the first flurry of shooting was over, the single birds would come flying out over the area where the mate had been dropped. Almost invariably you got that second bird. Don't know if they planned it that way or not.

"Another thing that Hanson tried, and we tried it too a little bit, trying to save crippled geese. You know, actually doctor 'em. Ran a hospital out here for a while to save cripples. I think they finally decided it was better to just let the geese heal themselves. So long as they were able to get to water, they would more or less survive. There are instances of a goose having a broken leg standing in one spot for several weeks until the leg healed. Of course, the problem with the cripples is predators. The concentration of birds around Horseshoe Lake has brought in more predators. And the balance of nature takes care of that. The raccoons get a lot of the real sick or hurt geese, and sometimes you see the mate of the cripple standing guard protectin' his mate. Funny thing is that a coon could actually clobber a goose if he knew it, but he doesn't know it. The goose can put up a big enough fight to scare the coon away. And I tell you, a goose has got a bill that can do you a lot of damage. Remember one day I caught a goose with my bare hands. Come up the back road into a field, and he was feeding in the corn; didn't see me, and I was downwind and everything else, and I ran up when he wasn't looking and grabbed him. Now it's a funny thing about a goose, when he knows you will catch him, he will stop running — a crippled goose, I've seen hunters chase 'em all over the field, their wing is broken, but nothing else is hurt; finally they run 'em down and when they got on top, the bird will set down and just let you pick him up.

"Well, that's what happened with this goose I caught in the cornfield, but when I picked him up he flapped his wings, and that hard joint in the wing slapped me right on my funnybone, and my arm was numb for a week.

"The geese aren't the only benefit at Horseshoe Lake. There are those bald eagles up there, a fairly large population, coons, and it's about the finest place for fishing; for bluegills, for bass — lots of fish in there, and in the summer you ought to see the visitors from Saint Louis, from Chicago, from all around the Middle West — how they come in there to camp and to fish. The geese manure that lake, and it's a great breeding ground for fish. The trouble with Horseshoe Lake is that it's subject to overflow every once in a while. The Mississippi River breaks in, and that brings in the rough fish; then they have to seine the lake and get as many of the rough fish out as they can.

"But the geese were always here; and in southwest Missouri, across the river, that was always nothin' but a big cypress swamp. It was just full of ducks and other birds; just full of 'em. But when they started to drain it off and cut the timber and that stuff, the birds got out, not nearly so many ducks there now.

"But if you want my opinion, I'd say that in the first place the politicians had a lot to do with starting these refuges — looked like they were trying to get rid of some cheap land and sell it to the state of Illinois. Had they known what was going to happen, the state, I mean, they probably wouldn't ever have created the refuge. Because the first parcel of land they acquired was total twenty-three hundred acres — that many birds on that much land is a problem. Now, of course, they have more'n eight thousand acres. But not at first. You do run into a conflict even now, a tremendous conflict, because these birds do do vast damage to farmers' crops. Sure, if you wanted to, and some do want to, you could build the flock up to a half-million birds; but if you did, you'd ruin the countryside.

"Now I want to tell a story. And this actually happened on our farm: we'd had a bad fall, harvestwise. We put two combines into a twenty-six acre field of soybeans. We were going to start to harvest the next morning. It rained that night, and it rained for four days; and in that four day period the geese got all the crop — every bean. *They* harvested the crop.

"But we operated the biggest hunting club down here. It was my father's farm. He bought it in 1904, or somewhere in there. It was a seven-hundred acre farm along the lake, and later we bought another. Then the preserve was established about 1927-28. When that happened, the clubs began to operate. The man who was on our farm says, 'We got more geese here than all the others put together; why don't we go into business?' So we started a hunting club about 1932 or 1933. We operated it roughly through the 1946 season. It was a very successful operation.

"And it puts to mind another thing; I talked just the other day with a kid from the Department of Conservation, Dave Kennedy. He and I agreed that there was a change between the hunters of today and the ones I was familiar with when we operated our club. The hunters in those days tended to be a little bit more sportsmanlike. They just never took advantage of the game and followed the rules of good sportsmanship. I had an orthopedic surgeon, Saint Luke's Hospital in Chicago. He had hunted all over the world. He made the observation that goose hunters tended to be larger and fatter than the average hunter. They tended to be obese. Maybe that is because they can stand in one spot and shoot, don't have to scratch and walk like they had to in the old days.

"We charged the hunters who came to our club seven dollars a day to hunt, and ten dollars a day if they wanted room and board. We had at our place seventeen full-time employees: cooks, chambermaids, guides, various people. We had a clubhouse where we could sleep thirty-two. Everybody that came to hunt got a breakfast consisting of a half grapefruit, all the bacon and eggs you could eat, and all the hot biscuits. It was a beautiful breakfast. Everybody thought it was wonderful. It was served every morning, and usually we'd serve forty, or fifty, or sixty people a day. I can remember when they used to set aside four or five pullman cars here at North Cairo. A group of hunters would come down, take over an entire pullman. I remember one group from Anderson, Indiana. They had two pullmans, and they went out of here with more geese than they could even think of liftin', and they raised the windows on the women's lavatory, so that the geese would keep until they got back to Indiana. That was the day that a fellow named "Too-Tall" Yates, he used to be clerk of our Circuit Court, he was one of our guides, had a little set-to with the Indiana crowd. They had got themselves all drunked up the night before, real drunk, and not a one of 'em was fit to hunt. So they asked Yates and me to kill the geese for 'em. Too-Tall got seventy-five birds, and I got forty-five. We killed a hundred and twenty geese. I shot off my left shoulder, and you won't believe *this*. I haven't even bought a duck stamp in ten years. I just want to go out and look at 'em now. I get just as much fun out of watching, now, and I love the birds in a way I guess I never did in the old days.

"Well, anyway, I shot off my left shoulder, and I never used a pad, I just had a light sweater and a huntin' coat on. But when that day's shooting was over I was black and blue from all the way around here down to *here*.

"But I'll tell you another thing, too. In all the years that we operated our club nobody was ever hurt. There was never an unfortunate discharge of firearm, and there was never some hunter that shot when another man was too close. We never had an accident at our club in all the years we operated. We had some drunks that got in a fight, but we didn't figure that was our responsibility. And another problem, you know, I'm a lawyer, and when a hunter'd get in jail we'd have to get him out, if we could. Well, they were able to carry things on pretty high. The largest pot I ever saw in a poker game, I saw at our club one night. That pot had over seven thousand dollars in cash. That pot was won by a judge of the Circuit Court of the state of Illinois. I was sitting behind him. I wasn't in the game; and that judge won that pot and bluffed it to win.

"If you wanted categories of people for our club, you'd find a large number of judges, lawyers, and doctors, and business executives. But you'd also find a number of coal miners to whom the ten dollar fee was significant. But they were real hunters, and they came down for a combination: to have some sport and to get a little extra food to eat. And another category is the local people who've been used to doin' this. We had a policy at the club that, except for Saturdays and Sundays, just call us up and if there was a vacant place, a vacant pit, they could come and hunt. But they didn't get the choice pits. We had probably twenty-five percent of the people who shot on our place, shot free of charge. The local folks.

"Don't forget now, Cairo itself is a river town, and all river towns tend to be wide open. Shawneetown, up the river here, is still a frontier town as far as I'm concerned. Saturday night in Shawneetown is just like 'Gunsmoke,' in my opinion. But in Prohibition times, we didn't have too much bootleggin' in this county. There was a lot of bootleggin' over here in western Kentucky, and in fact, there's a place just a few miles east of Paducah called Golden Pond, and they made so much bootleg whiskey that 'Golden Pond Bootleg Whiskey' was almost a brand name. But the big stills in this area were up along the river north of Metropolis, place up there, Brookport, where you go up the river, and you used to average a still a mile.

"Say, did you ever notice this? That geese always land downwind? They always, just before they let down, come into the wind, I don't care what direction they come from, unless it's absolute dead air. Geese are the great respecters of the law of aerodynamics. Did you know that at Horseshoe Lake is one of the finest stands of cypress in the state of Illinois, and one of the finest in the entire country? You remember when Sinclair Oil used to advertise what the world looked like long, long ago? Well, my brother used to say that out at Horseshoe Lake, that's what the world used to look like.

"Well, there was a doctor from Chicago who came down onetime with us. He was by himself, so we put one of these coal miners in the same pit with him. As a result of that acquaintance, for years thereafter that doctor took the coal miner on hunting trips with him. Paid all the bills. He and the doc hit it off perfectly. Shows you don't all have to have the same kind of education, long as you like to hunt and be a good sportsman. Doc insisted on good sportsmanship.

"I recall another time: after the hunters had all gone to the field, this very attractive lady showed up. She was the wife of a doctor who was out hunting. I gathered that she wasn't quite sure that he was on a hunting trip. So she had decided to follow him a little bit to see if he really *was* on a hunting trip. So, I had a station wagon, first station wagon in this area. I said, 'Come with me, I'll just drive you up, and you don't even need to talk to your husband. I'll point out where they are and everything.' Well, on the way up — huntin' was good that day, we went up where the hunters were, and I showed her just where her husband was and everything. We stood around up there for a while watching everything; and as we drove back down, there waitin' by the road, was a Dutchman from the Belleville area and an Evangelical Lutheran preacher. The limit was three geese a day, I can remember that. Flight of six geese had come over, and the preacher and the Dutchman got all six of 'em. And there, all of a sudden, they had their six geese, and they was wanting a ride back to the clubhouse. They got

in, and this lady, it was cold that day, and she was shiverin' a little bit. So this fellow, this Dutchman, he came up out of his pocket with a pint of whiskey. Well, he handed it to the lady and says, 'Ma'am, you ought to take a couple of pulls. It'll help the chill.' And she jerks away and says, 'Oh, no, I couldn't ever do that.' And he says, 'Oh well, then we'll git it blessed for you.' So he hands it to the Evangelical preacher, and he takes a pull out of it and hands it back to the lady, and of course, then, she took a couple of what I'd call very warmin' swallows and seemed to feel better about everything, husband and all.

"Remember another thing. We had a little barn up at the north end, where we would put our cars out of sight so there'd be no reflection, to scare the geese, and one day, it's about five minutes before shooting is over, and one of our guides is standing there just talking to me, he sees this lone goose coming. This guide says, 'I'm gonna get that goose.' He runs and gets his gun from the other end of that barn, puts in one shell, comes runnin' out and gets that goose. That's the way it was those days.

"We used to keep studies on moonlight, temperature, and weather conditions, fog even. But the big kill of geese came when the geese were hungry. If the birds are hungry it doesn't make any difference whether its rainin', sleetin', snowin', or is a hot day. Hunger was the thing that caused the birds to just come right in. I reached the conclusion that weather conditions just didn't have too much to do with it. Fog, you might say, was an exception, and the reason that fog was an exception was you could see the shadows of the birds. You could see them, and they couldn't see you. You could get 'em that way. It's kind of ghostlike shootin', shootin' geese in a fog.

"I remember one fellow we had. He was an executive of a big corporation. He didn't really come down here to hunt geese, but just to fetch a great big drunk. He was a constant problem around, and finally we had to bar him off of the place. But this one particular time he got in a fight. I had to get him out of the jail and into the hospital. He still had one goose with him. They couldn't make him let go of it. And later he goes to a convention at the Jefferson Hotel, in Saint Louis, still wearin' his huntin' clothes and still carryin' that damn goose. And there were, like that guy, a few hunters that we used to bar off our place. They were either sky-busters all the time, or just general disciplinary problems. We just barred 'em off. Life is too short to bother with those people.

"One thing we never, never did, though. We never served wild goose at the club table. That was not kosher. You couldn't do it then, and you can't do it now. We could furnish the facilities to get the geese killed, we'd draw 'em, and dress 'em, but we couldn't eat 'em on the property.

"But one of the side issues down here, is that there are a lot of these goose pickers who make darn good money, and they sell the feathers, too. Goose feathers bring a darn good price. Big problem is to get enough of 'em. But there's some of these pickin' places and sheds out there where they sell a lot of feathers. In the old days, they used to charge a standard price of about a buck to draw and pick a goose. Then they began to get machine pickers. Joe Hanna, a Syrian, he had a poultry business. And he did a big hunter's business, drawin', pickin', and freezin' geese. He'd pack 'em, too, ready for you to take 'em with you. Any given time he'd have maybe six hundred geese in there. And of course, he was always bein' checked to high heaven by federal agents and everybody else.

"But the last real contact I had with the goose-shooting industry was when a client of mine, ran a hunting operation, got charged with having a baited field. We tried his case, and he was found not guilty. I proved that the United States Government had stretched the truth some. In fact, the man who made the charge against my client has been demoted and taken out of the field. But we spent five hours trying that case before a United States magistrate.

"Well, when we were operating the club, we had a seventy-day season, and I'd be up every mornin' at four o'clock; then after things were goin' good, I'd come back to town and practice law and do my correspondence; then I'd go back in the afternoon after the shooting was over, make the settlement with the club manager, all that sort of stuff — there was a lot of cash layin' around, and we didn't want somebody to come in and rob us. And for seventy days I would get up every morning at four o'clock and rarely get to bed before midnight. Then lots of times, when the train would come in from Chicago, she'd get here about ten o'clock at night; we had to take five or six cars down there to just get our hunters off of the train.

"Tell you another thing. My father never shot a goose in his life. He owned the Lansden Farms Hunting Club. But he never hunted a goose, nor shot a goose. But it was funny, when he was out there visiting with the hunters, he could tell 'em how to do it. How to lead 'em, size of shot, the techniques, and all that sort of stuff. He could talk to you, and when he got through talkin', you would have thought he was the greatest authority on hunting that ever walked the earth. And he never owned a shotgun. Never had a taste for it — and maybe it was just because he felt something about the birds — I don't know."

"Funny thing about the oak trees at Horseshoe Lake, said Bob Lansden, as he and Joe sat over coffee, "the oaks are not reseeding themselves, because the geese eat all the acorns. Interesting sidelight, maybe.

"But you know, geese are surely creatures of habit. I learned that first from Jack Miner. That's why they go to the same places every year, and that's why it took so long for the dispersal program to get started. Jack Miner once told me, up at Kingsville, Ontario, at the refuge there, that his refuge was in operation three years before the first goose ever stopped. The first small flock actually stopped there by accident, twenty-some birds. That's all he had the first year. Next year he had a couple of hundred. And after that they came in the thousands. Miner also altered the migration habits of the geese by putting in the refuge at Kingsville. And I'll tell you another thing. It's only a one-day flight from Jack Miner's refuge in Ontario to Cairo and Horseshoe Lake; because one day on our refuge, or club, we killed seventeen banded birds, all of which had been banded the previous day at Kingsville.

"Jack Miner also told me of an incident where he banded two birds at ten o'clock one morning, and at four o'clock the following afternoon they were shot in Saskatchewan, twelve hundred miles from where he had banded them. Average of forty miles an hour. I talked to a Northwest Airlines pilot; during the war, I was flyin' from Seattle to Minneapolis, then goin' on to Washington — come in on Northwest Airlines. I asked this pilot if he saw many geese during the flights. He said he sure had to watch out for 'em during migration, and he had often asked the Civil Aeronautics Administration to give permission to go up or down according to the altitude the birds were flyin'. Well, the migrations from north to south, when the flock starts movin', it comes fast! I figure that geese do cruise at approximately forty miles an hour.

"Was a time the birds flew straight to Horseshoe Lake. But when they put in the Horicon Marsh refuge, it altered their migration patterns. I would think this: that it wouldn't be unusual for those geese to fly out of James Bay nonstop to Cairo. We could always tell when the flights were comin' in from the north. The flights would have a larger number of birds in 'em. They'd be makin' a lot of noise. Their wings were fluttering. They always came in high when they came in from the north, and you could see their wings, and they fluttered their wings, and they were makin' lots and lots of noise. The leader, his neck and head were almost twistin' off to make sure that they were in the right spot. I was out onetime with a fellow who was born in Germany and worked for Count Zeplin, you know, the lighter-than-air inventor. And after World War I, they actually flew Zeplins commercially to Scandinavia. This fellow was out with me one day hunting, 1940 or 1941, he was a consultant for the United States Navy. It was one of these beautiful days when the geese were flying everywhere and all real high, and I remember him makin' the remark, 'It's just like it was in Scandinavia.' That's the surprising thing in the European zoos. You see geese that are just like these geese here.

"And of course, there's the famous Himalayan Flyway, you know, where the geese go down the Volga Flyway to the Himalaya Mountains and fly right over them.

"The geese tend not to come down to Horseshoe Lake until the bitter weather drives 'em down. The geese start comin' in here, you know, about the middle of September. They start leavin' around the first of April. That's somethin' to notice, too, when they start gettin' restless, when the migratory urge is gettin' into 'em.

"Jack Miner used to put a verse from the Bible on every goose band. There's lots of Bible verses that only contain three or four words: 'Follow me,' 'I am the Way.' He once got an award from the United Council of Churches, as having been one of the most effective spreaders of Christianity. That was because the Indians would shoot the banded bird, and they would see the writing on it. They'd take the band to the missionary. He'd translate it, and soon have them converted.

"You were askin' about Prohibition days down here, and that reminds me that in March of 1973, I was appointed to defend a guy in federal court. Charge: bootleggin'! I'm happy to report that the jury was out all of twelve minutes and acquitted him.

"And here's another thing we noticed. The birds now are starting to fly over Cairo, now that the season is over. They go into Kentucky just across the river here. And that will be a significant thing all winter: the birds commuting across the river between Horseshoe and the Kentucky area. They go because they've probably eaten up everything around Horseshoe Lake. You simply couldn't raise enough feed for all their requirements. But I'll tell you one thing. They used to say, you know, that geese didn't hurt winter wheat; but I'll tell you, they clean out a wheat crop here. We used to plant wheat to attract the geese into our fields but we never harvested it. They got it all. Every leaf.

"We had once eleven hundred acres right in there around Horseshoe Lake. We sold that off to the state of Illinois. It was a profitable enterprise. We had some of the really vital acres, and the Wicker Club near us had them too. There were twenty-seven acres right in the choice part, and I venture to say that there were more geese shot over that twenty-seven acres than anyplace in North America.

"And you talk about the economics of goose hunting. The smallest expenditure that any hunter sustained was the daily fee paid to the hunting club; because he had his transportation, his entertainment; because they enjoyed themselves, and they spent a lot of money. They went to garages to get their cars fixed or washed after bein' out in the mud. Then there was the actual shootin', the number of shells they shot. Well, most hunters just aren't very good shots. I would say that the average hunter takes twenty-five shells to kill two geese. I came up with a figure which I think was low. It was that every goose killed in Alexander County represented an expenditure of forty dollars per goose, figure into the number of birds killed; and that figure was higher than any payroll in industry in Alexander County. I would say now that the figure is doubled. The figure might be a hundred dollars per bird. That might be what it costs to kill one bird.

"Just figure it out. A fellow lives in Chicago, and he drives a car down here. He is gone from home four days, and he spends two of those four days here. And he goes out of here with say, four geese. It wouldn't be hard to say a hundred dollars a bird.

"What I am trying to convey is that it's not just the club operators who have a good thing. It is a basic industry to the whole community. Seventy days a year. But during that seventy days it really pumps money into this community. Well, the liquor is pretty good, too. Some of that is defensive, of course. It's a good form of antifreeze. You stand in a pit — that's why they drink Scotch whiskey in Scotland, to keep from freezin' to death.

"But we haven't operated a huntin' club since the year 1946. I don't believe there's been a year since the time we stopped, that I haven't had a request from a former hunter of ours to get him a place to hunt. Oh, I had one this year."

"Mister Lansden, I hunted on your place in the old days. Haven't been there in several years. Can you get me a place to hunt?"

"I got a call one day, about four o'clock in the afternoon from a lawyer in Peoria."

He said, "I'm leavin' Peoria now. I want to go huntin' in Cairo for two days, and I need a reservation."

"Well," I says, "You're assumin' that I can do it."

"Oh," he says, "you can do it. You find me a place to hunt, so when I get to Cairo around eleven o'clock tonight, I'll call you and find out where I'm supposed to go."

"Well, he called, and he was called, and he was callin' from a nightclub. Had a bunch of strippers and B-girls, and all that sort of stuff, and I says, well, it sounds like you have arrived. He says, 'Yeah, I'm out at the Highway Club;' and I says, all right you're staying out at Ferris Club, and I told him how to get there. Well it so happened, that the next day there was a lawyer friend of mine down here. He and I were on a case. He had never seen the hunting, and so we got up early and went out and had breakfast at one of the places where they serve it: all you can eat for two dollars or three dollars, used to be a buck, you know. We had breakfast, then we visited some of the clubs, and went over to the Ferris Club, and here come these two guys out in the field. They have already got their two geese, and it's then about nine o'clock."

"Well, howdy Bob, good to see you. You sure fixed us up fine. Wonderful and everything else."

I says, "Did you have a good time? And just for my information, how much did that evening cost you?"

"Oh," he says, "about two hundred dollars."

And I says, "what are you going to do tonight?"

And he says, "Why, going back to the Highway Club."

"Now I tell you, that's another thing that some of this nightlife did. I think that some guys came down from pretty conservative communities. Never saw anything like it is here. And their visit to Cairo is a conversation piece to 'em for the rest of the winter. It's something that's part of the game.

"Now I did have a friend that lived in Glenview, Illinois. He used to spend all winter down in his basement practicin' duck callin' and goose callin'. His wife damn near went crazy. She heard geese comin', goin' and every other which way. Tell you a funny story about a goose call. Onetime I was in Chicago with my son, then about twelve or thirteen. He had a little sister who was then about five. Well, he and his friends wanted to see the Chicago Blackhawks, hockey, and this was New Year's Eve. Well, I said, I'll take you all down, the game will be over, and we'll be home long before midnight. You know, when the Blackhawks play there's always a lot of noise going on. So I just handed my young daughter a Martin goose call we had layin' around the house; and there's all this noise goin' on down there, and suddenly there is a lull. It's quiet, and at that moment this young daughter of mine chose to let fly on this goose call. And everybody in the whole place looked around, wonderin' where that darn goose was at. Thought there was a wild goose flyin' around the Chicago Stadium. In fact, my son is now out in California. I bought him a goose call and sent it out to 'im. One of Ken Martin's. In fact, Ken used to be on our place. He was just a farmer then, tinkerin' with those calls. He was on our farm at that time.

"Another strange thing. When they put the closed zone in, you could shoot ducks in the zone, but you couldn't shoot geese. The most fantastic duck hunting I ever had in my life; there was a blizzard comin' in, and we went into those woods. It snowed like the duce that night, and the next day we drove up in a wagon and tractor through snow up to your hips. We got into the same place, and we managed to get in two more hours of good huntin' until the weather got so bad the ducks just wouldn't fly anymore. That was in the closed zone. Incidentally, the farmer who drove the tractor was the one I defended in 1973 — you know.

"Now, from the aesthetic standpoint, I think I get an unending pleasure, on a nice still calm, sunny fall afternoon; and we have a gorgeous climate here, finest climate in the world, from first of October till the middle of November. I love to go out to one of those places along the lake bank at Horseshoe Lake and see those geese work. Never fails to satisfy me, I remember onetime I was handling a federal estate tax return for an estate that I represented. This internal revenue agent called and said he was dissatisfied with some of the valuations we had placed on the farmland. He thought it was much too high. Well, I said, if you are comin' to Cairo, we'll go out there. Well, on the way from Cairo to this farm, we went by Horseshoe Lake, and the geese were just flyin' around, and I said, if we finish our trip in time we'll stop here on the way back. So I took him up to this farm. Went all over it, so he could see just what the character of the drainage was, sloughs, and all this sort of stuff. Then we came back and pulled in there by the landing by the island, and we just sat down. We sat there and just watched the birds. And it was just gorgeous! They came within twenty feet of us. We didn't say much to each other. We just enjoyed ourselves. Then we got in the car, and as I started up, driving to the driveway before I got to the highway, he says, 'Mister Landsen, I'm gonna accept that return!'

"Once in a while Horseshoe Lake freezes over. To me that's one of the funnier sights. This business does have some comic aspects, too. When a goose lands on the ice, he skids! Then he gets up. He is the most embarrassed-lookin' thing you ever saw. They hit the ice and skid!

"Well, I guess we've about run out the string, but one more story. Once we had on the farm a state policeman. Every year he'd ask my father, 'Can I bring the big shots down? Eight or ten of 'em, want 'em to go huntin'.' "

"Sure," my father says, "glad to have you do it. Bring 'em around. We'll take 'em to dinner, that sort of stuff."

"Well, one particular day hunting was over seven or ten minutes, a flock of geese went over the place where these troopers were, they shot and killed a bunch of 'em. There was a warden right there in this barn, and he hollers, 'Oh, that's a terrible violation of the law,' and he jumps in his car and rushes over there. About ten minutes later, the warden came back. Didn't have much to say or anything. But later when I saw this trooper I says, what happened?"

"Oh," he says, "you'll get a laugh out of this. This fellow came stormin' up and yellin', 'let me see your license. This is the most terrible violation of the law I ever seen,' and the commanding officer of the state police says, 'Hey, by the way, we're sort of in the business of checkin' licenses ourselves. We'd like to see *your* drivin' license.' "

"And the guy didn't have one. That's where it became a tie. The case was settled out of court."

In southern Illinois, Alexander County, at the beginning of the present century, there were comparatively few goose hunters, because goose hunting was no sport for the novice. Most of the hunters were skilled river men; those who traveled to the hunting grounds by land did so by horse- or mule-drawn vehicles over many tiresome miles of nearly impassable roads. Once at the shooting grounds, there remained the task of digging a pit and placing the decoys. After a hard day's hunt, the hunter either camped out on a bare sandbar, or faced a long return trip. Although there were more geese and fewer hunters in those early days, real skill was required to bag geese consistently, because the goose range was extensive and the sandbars numerous.

Then, as now, silhouettes, or "shadows," as they are called locally, were used to decoy the geese. "Shadows" are one-dimensional cutouts painted to resemble geese. Live decoys were seldom used until after 1906, when it became the custom to use three live decoys in combination with the silhouettes. The silhouettes were arranged in V-formation, with the apex of the V downwind from the pit. A live "caller" was placed at the vertex and at each end of the V. In between were the "shadows." Bait was not used, but, in order to induce the geese to work into the proper bar, hunters sometimes placed scarecrows on adjacent bars.

Improved roads and faster transportation brought goose hunting within the reach of the masses. Heavy competition for the better hunting places ensued. The demand for more hunting grounds resulted in the development of field shooting.

Long before baiting came into prominence,

goose hunters recognized that no other type of feed was more attractive to geese than a large field of fall-planted wheat or rye. As soon as the weather turned cold, however, shelled and ear corn, wheat kernels, cowpeas, and similar feeds, when properly scattered, proved very attractive to the geese, although their desire for greens continued.

When live decoys were used, the usual procedure was to construct a pen using a roll or two of three-foot wire. In this pen were placed as high as one hundred geese. Usually one or more geese were separated from their mates so that they would "talk" back and forth to each other. Another trick was to place a trained goose, which was wing clipped, in the blind; the goose was then thrown from the blind and permitted to walk to the pen, "talking" to its mate in the pen as it went. If the first decoy failed to entice a wild flock within the range of the gunner, others were released from the pit until the wild geese were decoyed as desired, or the supply of decoys was exhausted. Only a small percentage of captive geese behaved in such a manner as to make good decoys. These geese became as valuable an aid in goose hunting as well-trained bird dogs are in quail hunting, and commanded equally high prices on the market. The function of live decoys was to attract the geese, while that of feed was to hold them and to encourage the birds to return again.

One answer to increased hunting pressure was the formation of goose hunting clubs, but since the time of the Egyptian Hunting and Fishing Club, organized in 1904, goose clubs changed considerably in Alexander County. Present-day clubs, with a few exceptions, are strictly commercial. In contrast, this first club (which had annual dues of only five dollars), was a nonprofit organization. At onetime, it boasted a membership of fifty, all local hunters. In 1941, there were at least two dozen clubs in Alexander County, each of which, according to a direct comparison of kill records, killed more geese annually than did the Egyptian Club.

Goose hunting first took on a commercial aspect when in 1913 a Chicago businessman began to lease the sandbars most frequently used by the geese. By 1916, most of these bars were no longer open to public hunting. Up to that time, field shooting had been scorned by most real goose hunters. Now that the river shooting was largely under the control of a few men, it was field shooting or nothing for the old-timers.

The purchase of Horseshoe Lake for a refuge in 1927 created a boom in commercialization of goose shooting. Mediocre farmlands located near the refuge suddenly commanded fancy prices. Almost every field located around the refuge contains pits and blinds during the hunting season.

In the darkness of the early southern Illinois morning, the three men crawled into the goose pit. The pit was a trench, really, about eight feet long, six feet wide, and perhaps seven or eight feet deep. At the front, nearest the lake, was a kind of roof, or cover. Under this cover was a long bench, and at the rear wall was a sort of step on which one stood to shoot.

It was a little like, if one exercised a bit of imagination, trenches in the Civil War, or maybe in World War I, complete with earthworks, places to stand when firing at the enemy. The geese, of course, represented no enemy, but they definitely played the role of an antagonist — something to be competed against, a laurel to be won, or to satisfy the so-called primitive urge that propelled thousands of men into the geese pits, into the woods for deer, onto the lakes for ducks, into the cornfields for pheasant, and into the night woods for raccoon.

The arrangement — the men, grunting and mostly silent so early in the morning, and their weapons, held against the slow dim light as they climbed into the trench, was like an unorganized military operation. It wasn't military, and yet it was, too, in the marshalling of weapons and shells, the rations: largely coffee and liquor, of course, but still rations, and the place of campaign.

The pit was relatively simple. Standing forward, under the roof, or cover, a man was hidden from any goose flying above. There was a small heating stove in the pit, where, on really cold mornings, a small fire could be made and hands kept warm. This morning there was no fire, and the pit was damp and gloomy.

Far out on the lake the occasional voices of calling geese could be heard. They were still resting; there had been no sign whatever of flight as yet, and the men mumbled, wondering when, how many, how high. They muttered about the wind; it had been blowing strong late in the night, but seemed pretty calm now. There was little movement on the water. Faintly, in the far distance there came a rumble of traffic; for the noise of the trucks and autos was impossible to shut out. Somebody remarked on this; how nice it would be if there were no car noises; but where could one go to get away from them?

The goose calls from the lake were rather subdued; not of geese about to take off in flight, said one of the men. It was more like the calls of mated geese talking to each other, or calling each other back when they strayed too far away. It was, if one shut his eyes, a gratifying wild sound, and the walls of the blind took away the wildness, of course, and put the whole thing almost on a commercial basis; for a heavy price had been paid for the blind, and for the right to use it for a few hours.

As the light grew, the decoys could be seen on the field in front. The corn had all been knocked down, the stubble lying broken over, falling every which way, and the leaves dangling, whispering a little in the slow, morning wind.

The stuffed decoys, about thirty of them, were placed out in front, and the scene, in the early morning, was eerie, unreal, a crass, yet fantastic make-believe.

Now and again a single goose would rise a

few feet from the lake, honking, and drop back, landing at a location a few rods away, almost as though trying wings. Soon small groups, possibly family groups, gander, goose, and some of the young from the past summer's mating, would take off, rise, circle, and drop back, or head out toward a feeding ground. Finally, a flight rose and came high over the blind. The men waited tensely, conjecturing in short, excited sentences about the direction, the height at which the birds were flying. One of the men raised his shotgun, a Western Field pump, twelve gauge, and one of the others spoke to him quietly, saying that the birds were much too high to hit. The first man argued, wanted to fire, but did not, and the flight passed over.

In about twenty minutes, three birds started from the lake and flew toward the blind. These were definitely lower than the other flight. All three men now got ready, shotguns poised, and the geese came very fast, and from below they seemed huge and very near.

"Let them have it," said the man with the pump gun, and all three blazed away, several shots upward. The three birds seemed to turn and bounce in air and veered away, wings beating at twice the tempo of before the shots, and flew away seemingly uninjured.

The men fell immediately to wondering why, what was the matter, was the load too light; why didn't they get all three birds?

They reached the conclusion, which a better judge of distance and one with experience could have told them instantly, that the distance was too great; that the birds seemed nearer than they were, and that at about ninety yards away, which is roughly what the birds were, hardly any guns would bring them down.

The men said nothing at all about the shot that might have struck into the feathers of the geese; or that some of it must have stayed there.

So the day, the morning went on. Between small flights, all too high to shoot at, the men had coffee from a thermos, and later in the morning, shots from a bottle of Old Southern Crow that one of them had brought.

No geese were struck, and at the other blinds, which couldn't be seen in the early morning, but of which there were many throughout the field, nobody else seemed to be having luck either.

About eleven o'clock, when it began to look as though there would be no geese taken, the men began to fire at anything that came over, no matter how far away. The guns blazed and blasted, and finally, about two o'clock when they were talking about quitting for the day, a wounded bird flew unevenly toward their blind. The goose was coming down, struggling to keep going, but losing altitude. He had been shot somewhere else, perhaps a couple of miles away. As he came within definite range, all three hunters took him, blasting several shots, and the torn bird struck the cornfield directly in front of the blind.

One of the men, the one with flowered hunting cap, leapt out and seized the dead bird, holding it aloft. It was broken, dirty, bloody, and pathetic, but the three hunters who had come out from Saint Louis shouted in victory and suggested that a round of Old Southern Crow would go very, very well.

At one time, there were no geese here at all. I recall the morning I saw the first big flock in a cornfield.

The peace of the countryside becomes complete when the birds return.

At the Horseshoe Lake refuge in southern Illinois, the wild geese group by family, by father, mother and offspring hatched in the nesting grounds in the far north. By family groups, the flock begins its northward migration. For some days now, the geese have sensed the changing patterns of the weather and have, by intuition and perhaps observation, read the far, high skies. They have fattened on the corn and on fields of greens planted by the refuge men; physically, the geese are in excellent condition. Those wounded during the hunting season have recovered, or, unable to fly, or hurt too badly to recover, have died; some have been killed and eaten by the eagles or foxes, and others have made their peace with the waters and the land of the refuge, and they will stay. Perhaps a few will even mate and raise young. But the great combined family of the flock will depart.

The signs are in the sky and upon the land. There is a sensation of the vague new spring. The days have lengthened, and within the bodies of the birds there are subtle changes. An impelling urge grows daily. On their way to and from the cornfields, picked clean now and gleaned over and over, the flock flies high, higher than during the hunting season, even, higher by far than on their daily trips from the roosting grounds to feed. There is a great restlessness in the group atmosphere. Families circle and move within the larger groups of birds resting on the pasture slopes. Mates stay close together, and last season's young birds follow and wait.

Until by some signal, or impelling and irresistible urge, the first portions of the flock take to the high air. The leader points north, and behind him the V's of the flyers form. There are muted voice communications. The birds in the high air wheel slowly, and on the ground the restless flock feels similar urges. Family by family, group by group, they take to the sky, and like a great funnel from the earth, the migration begins. Little by little they join and join again; at times the sky seems black with flight. The line of the migration stretches forward and back, and on the ground, at the refuges first, the men see the start and watch the feeding grounds empty of the flock. Among the men there is a feeling of sadness to see them go, for the birds, during the winter, have become a part of the men's daily life. They have counted from the airplane the numbers of birds on the refuges; they have worried about the food available, for this year there have seemed to be many more birds than ever before. The surrounding countryside has also felt the hard impact of the flock, and the fields have been shredded by the hungry, seeking bills. Many birds, during the winter, were trapped and banded, and the plastic strips around their neck, colored brightly, will identify certain birds and help keep an account of them as they may be captured elsewhere or perhaps killed by hunters.

The men of the refuges have grown very emotional about the birds. Often they will have identified certain members of the flock; and in a strange relationship, the men have grown emotionally close to the birds. They often mutter: "I hope you make it back, my friend. I hope you make it through another year, friend." And the muttered words, almost like a prayer, are sincere and deeply meant.

Now the migration north is in full flight. It

is not hurried, nor frantic, as may be the migration that comes from north to south. The northward migration is more leisurely. The flock will not hurry, for by some mysterious sense, the birds know that there is still frigid air at the nesting grounds and that there is deep snow, and likely that there will be blizzards. They will not hurry, hoping that when they arrive the weather will have turned, and the season of spring will be started. For food must be found there, too. And in the north, there are no refuges where corn is planted and winter wheat is green on many slopes and fields back away from the water.

Often, the northering flock will dawdle at locations on its migration. Certainly there will be stopovers at the Horicon Marsh where, again, they are expected; for the men of that marsh work by the seasons, with the arrival and with the departure of the flock.

At Horicon, the flock will eat whatever they can find, storing up strength and fat for the northward journey, and for the days when there will be little food.

Men below them throughout their northward journey will look into the sky, and marvel at the long lines and V's of the migration, and something will take place in them too. For the flock and the men are linked by urges too deep to identify. Men feel these same compelling flights that the flock feels. Men, restless, feel the urges to move, to migrate. In the rural areas throughout the whole nation, human families will by spring tradition make their annual move — from farm to farm, from dwelling to dwelling; for about March it has always been thus with birds and with men. Those men who remain in the same locations may also feel the dissatisfactions with their scene; they would like to move, to migrate, but the ties are too deep and too many. Nevertheless, the men are envious of the freedom of the flock to come, to go, to follow the seasons through the sky and upon the land.

Poets, as the birds move north, stare upward and feel the urges to make words into patterns of art; for the flock is inspirational, through nature, perhaps, through God. The grace, the outstretched necks, the mysterious, far cries, the wildness, the release of energy in beautiful action — these things the poets cherish.

Painters look long at the flights; and on the waters the painters will see how the birds come in, land, and in flight take off beating upward so easily, so rapidly. And on canvas the painters may record what they have seen — with birds, with the wildness of the scene, with evening skies — morning skies, with the water, with the movement, with the bodies.

The flock brings hope and release to prisoners confined in places over which the migration may pass. And the imprisoned people feel responses to the flock — to hope that freedom for them may follow, to appreciate, to see in the same way as the flock. Yes, the flight north, the migration in the spring, the return to the frozen ground, is different from the fall flight. It is filled with stranger impulses, for spring, and the rites of spring, have always been deep within the souls and spirits of animals, birds, and men. Celebrations must be made, strange music heard, movements of dance and flight initiated.

The Indians of the place of nesting along the shores and in wild country back from James Bay have suffered through the long, long winter. They have had food, but by early spring even it has grown very hard to obtain. The Indian women and the children complain and the men watch the skies for it is near the time of the arrival of the wild geese.

When the geese come in the spring, the men clean and ready their weapons; anyone who has a gun becomes a hunter. The food is necessary for the Indian people's survival, and they wait, a part of the cycle just as the geese themselves are compelled to return to the nesting grounds. The Indian women wait too, cooking utensils prepared, and the Indian children play games pretending that they are geese and hunters. It has been a very long and a hard winter. Sometimes, after a mild winter, the permafrost will melt farther below the surface of the great muskeg, as the nesting grounds is called; but that will not happen this year. There was much snow, and terrible cold. The Indian peoples suffered, and some of the old ones died. Now, with the advent of the geese, starvation will be ended.

Some of the older Indian men make up fantastic stories. The stories pass the time and sharpen anticipation for the goose hunts to come. Old La Boutille, ninety years old, sits in the doorway of his small house and tells about the year that there were no berries and no game. The children cried all day long, and the old men prepared themselves for their last sleep. And then suddenly, as the ice broke up, the geese arrived. They came nearer and nearer, a flock miles long, miles wide. Some of the great flock flew over and away; but many

alighted on the lake out from the settlement. They did not approach the shore, and no one knew how to take them. But the starving people must be fed.

Then to La Boutille came a great idea. He shouted to everyone to prepare many cords of babiche, each with a running noose at one end. While this was being done he procured a whip-like sapling. The cords were many, but light in weight, and he fastened them to his body. Dragging the stick, he plunged into the cold, cold waters of the lake and swam with all his might toward the flock of floating geese. As he neared them, he sank below the waters and swam underneath. He unfastened the cords, and with deft fingers, slipped a noose around each pair of legs within reach. Moving rapidly this way and that, he secured many, many birds until, his supply of babiche exhausted, he had captured as many birds as would form a feast for half the Indian peoples of the north.

Then up he popped in the midst of the still unknowing birds, and shouting, stirred the birds into wildest activity. With thunderous beating of wings, they rose clear of the water, and doing so, each bird tightened the cord on its leg. Up, up they flew, drawing old La Boutille with them into the sky.

He steered the geese steeds through the sky toward his settlement; and his hands, because of his terrible hunger, held the many reins like those of a racing chariot. As the strange flight came above the Indian settlement, La Boutille pulled in on the reins, and as goose after goose fell back within reach, he dealt it a thwack with his sapling. The bird fell to the length of its cord and acted as a brake for the entire flight. Then, as his lodge, surrounded by surprised faces, came into view, he pulled in hard on the cords attached to his remaining steeds. He dealt blows right and left with his cudgel. Each blow lessened the speed of the flight, and as the few supporting geese continued to struggle, La Boutille gradually descended, until, with the last few struggling birds, he landed gently on the earth before his teepee. So he told the story while they waited for the geese to come.

When the early returning geese have lingered on the shores or on the rivers, waiting for the breaking up of the ice, and when they have flown back and forth between the open places and the sedges where there may be berries remaining, the Indians will have reached the end of their own waiting. They set forth to hunt and take the geese if they can. It is not so simple as La Boutille's story and not so delightful. Often the birds are very wary and very hard to come close to. Sudden blizzards may thwart the hunters, so that in a whole day of hunting they may get not a shot at the geese. Also, the hunting is dangerous. The great muskeg is a vast water-logged plain 135,000 miles square. There are a few trees of stunted spruce and tamarack and areas of bog and pothole lakes. Floating masses of sedge and grasses cover much of the water area, and the surface of the sedges looks solid, too solid, for when the Indian steps carelessly upon it he may sink.

The Indians know the dangers, and they know the areas where they may safely step upon the surface; even so, some have perished in the cold waters.

The Indians hunt the geese with shotguns and with rifles, with sticks and stones, and with bare hands; for while the period of molting is on, when the birds have no feathers and cannot fly, they are vulnerable to the Indians.

It is possible to chase down and to capture a running goose. The mates, as they nest, are also in the molting stage, and they and their young are prey to the Indians — if they can be found. Not so many are captured by hand, for the terrain is far too uncertain; but on an island, or along the shore where there are rocks, birds can be trapped against walls, or chased among low grasses.

When the *niskapesim* or "goose moon" of the Crees is ended, there will be many Canada geese in the homes of the Indians — salted, and hanging, and the bones of hundreds of birds picked clean will be lying in refuse heaps.

And the young birds hatched in the spring, as they get feathers but before they fly in August, will be hunted and many taken by the Indians.

The Indians are not cruel. They love the geese and revere their presence. There is mystery, even religion, attached to the birds; and a great sadness falls upon the Indian peoples when the geese depart. Again, the winter will be long; food will certainly become scarce in the late winter months; and once again in March and April the Indians will scan skies for the return of the migration.

One Cree Indian whose family had nearly starved during a terrible winter of great snow set forth near the middle of May, hoping that the geese would be coming back. He would like to bring home several fat ones, expecting that the birds had eaten well on the refuges in America, and that they would be excellent nourishment for his hungry children and for the old members of his family. He went a long way, and the snows were as deep as at his home place. His hunting grounds were on the Lawapiskau River and the country adjacent to the river. He looked carefully, listened carefully, and could hear no sound of the geese. They were late, later than they had ever been in coming to the nesting grounds. Usually by May the birds were there, and usually there was goose to eat. When he got near the river, he searched carefully along the snow-piled banks. In the snow, nearly covered, he found the bodies of several geese, and along the bank several rods farther there were many others, He pried geese out of the snow and held them up. He could see that they were very, very thin. There was little flesh on their legs and the breasts felt scrawny. Their crops were completely empty. Slowly, he let the birds drop to the snow and turned back toward his camp. The geese had come too early and had starved to death. In the south they could not know that the Canadian winter had been the longest ever recorded.

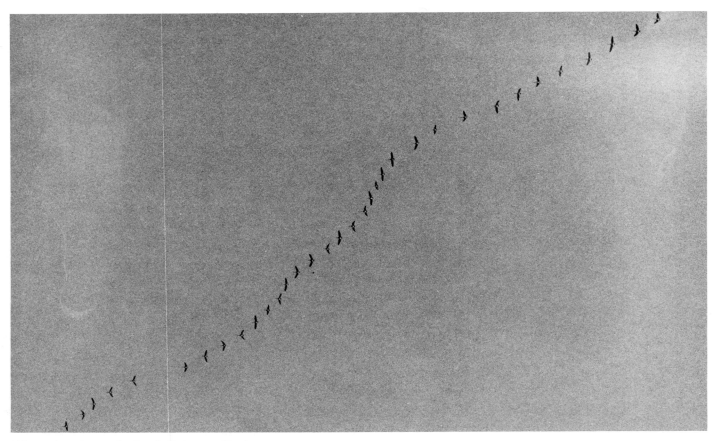

When they leave in the fall, I go with them.

When they come in the spring, I am there to meet them.

114

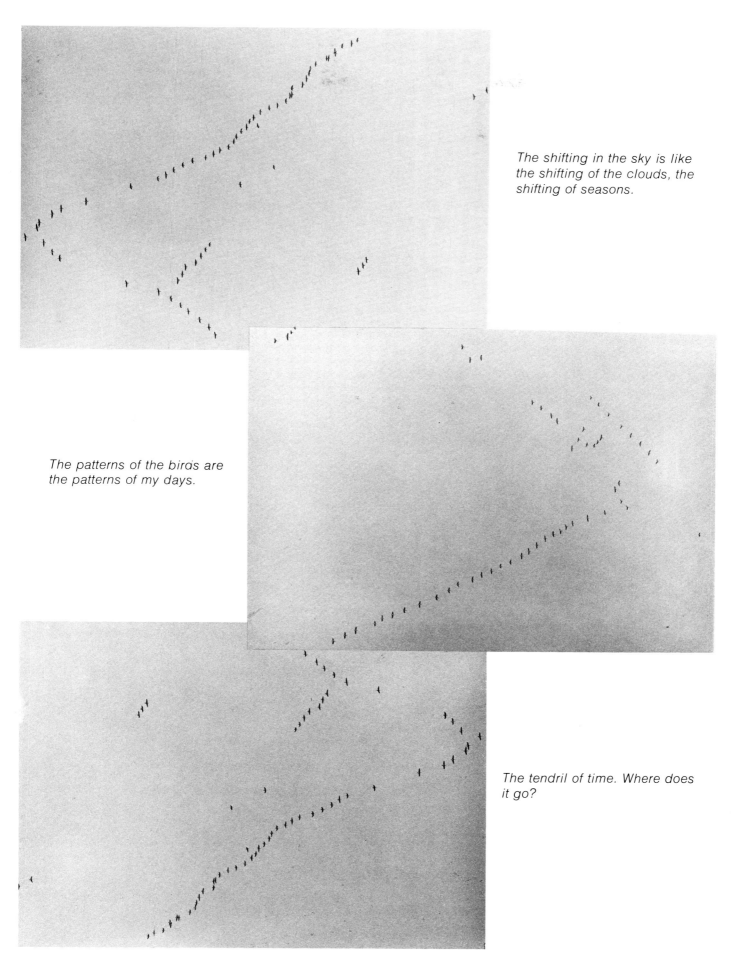

The shifting in the sky is like the shifting of the clouds, the shifting of seasons.

The patterns of the birds are the patterns of my days.

The tendril of time. Where does it go?

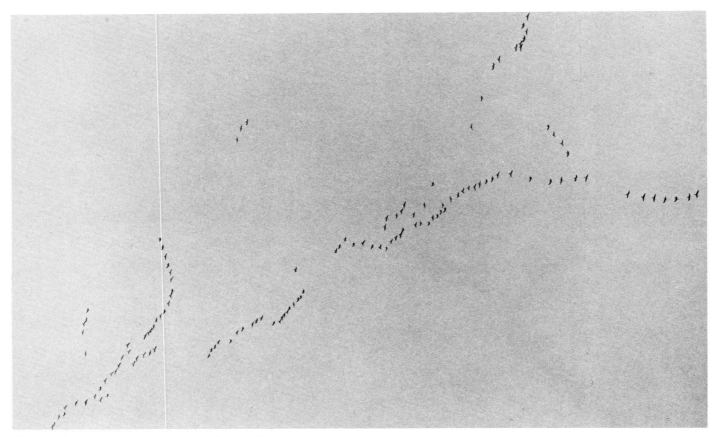

The wild geese weave the lace of primitive time.

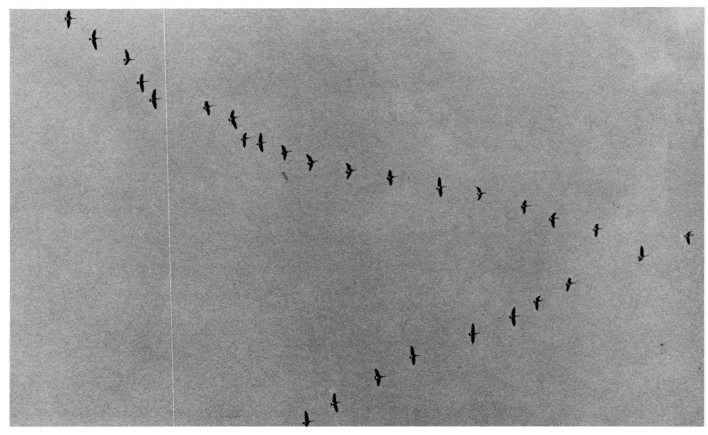

There is a mood I feel only when I see the Canadas stretched out across the vast gray of space.

116

Wild geese mate for life, among all the animals and birds, the wild geese are about the most faithful. There is little infidelity among them. They select, abide, and remain faithful until death. And perhaps untimely death does separate most wild geese — the blast of a hunter's gun on an early morning accounts for many missing mates. When pathetically, a hunter downs one of a flying pair, if he but waits it will almost always happen that the other, the bereft, will come back, flying over the same place where the mate was killed. Then, if the hunter is skillful and perhaps has pity in his heart for the frantic bird, he will send another charge upward, and the remaining one will plunge to join his mate. This has happened countless times and is part of the saga of every goose hunter.

It is certain that the members of the flock can identify their mates, even within a gathering of ten thousand geese all appearing much the same to human eyes. The gander walks directly to his mate, or the goose directly to the gander to whom she is wed. Perhaps this is done by certain special movements of the head; it is not done necessarily and solely by voice. It may be done by the way a particular bird stands, or walks, or by delicate individual markings which the goose will see and recognize, but which people do not ordinarily see.

There is a pecking order within the flock which regulates who can feed first and who goes where first, and possibly this has something to do with the mate selections. There is also great aggression among the males of the flock. The gander is a vigorous, arrogant, self-willed creature who must fight for his position and for his territory within the flock.

When nesting, the gander will not tolerate other males close by. His realm is his own, his and his mate's. He guards his mate on her nest and has firmly demarcated lines for his territory over which no other bird dare cross. He does little during the nesting process but guard, and feeds himself only, for the goose eats hardly at all during the nesting period. She loses weight daily, until, when her twenty-nine days are up, and the goslings have broken out of the shell, she may hardly be more than a skeleton of the fattened bird who came up from the southern refuges. And when the goslings have hatched and within a few minutes become able to stagger about, and within a few more minutes or an hour or so are actually able to leave the nest and get to the water, the gander circles nervously, watching, ready to defend against other birds or animals.

It is now that the mother goose will seek food for herself, and the little ones begin right away to seek insects, for they may subsist in their early life chiefly upon protein. The adult geese live upon green growth and seeds and roots.

The coming of the goslings to the water is a beautiful and rare sight. The goose has built her simple nest perhaps as high as she can — upon a rock or a hummock projecting above the surrounding water and land. And at times the location she has chosen is very high indeed. Members of the flock have sometimes built nests upon a cliff, or a very high projection of land, and when the goslings are hatched they must find their way downward to the water. Somehow, they are able to do this. The little ones come sliding and slipping, a comical sight if there is anyone to see, and the gander watches in apprehension. Perhaps he is not so much concerned about the small ones' ability to find their way, as he is concerned about the possible appearance of a predator. At any rate, the goose and her little brood do reach the water, join the gander, and the small family of five, six, or eight (perhaps many fewer at times) becomes a tightly held small entity.

Sometimes tragedy happens during the time of the nesting. The eggs, for instance, may be infertile, or a sudden freeze, if the nesting is too early, has come to destroy the fertility of the eggs. The goose continues to sit, and she will sit until the eggs hatch, or if they do not, she may continue to sit for days longer than her span.

When this occurs, the goose might actually starve. It has happened many times; and the gander, not understanding why the waiting is so long, continues his vigil even after his mate is dead.

He will, of course, eventually join the flock on its southern migration, but he remains at the nesting site long, long after the mate is dead. He may join the many single geese who have their own territory at the nesting grounds removed from the nesting sites of the pairs. And he will fly with these groups, with the singles, and eventually he may take another mate. He will never do so while his mate is still alive.

The goose, during the nesting, has laid an egg a day, until the clutch is complete. Then she will begin her long sitting on the nest so that the eggs will all hatch at the same time. When this happens, it becomes very important that the little goslings find adequate food, for they must grow rapidly. The time of the migration will not allow for much leisure. They must be grown, feathered, tried in flight before the time, for the family will remain together during the southern migration and during the time at the refuge grounds during the winter. They remain together if they survive the southern hunting season, and eventually the young join in the regular and fascinating cycle of mating, nesting, and growth. Here are some other observations, gleaned from many sources, about Canada geese.

Fear of man is not intuitional. It has to be learned from experience. They learn this very rapidly.

To young geese, the mother is their leader until they are about three weeks old. Geese "talk" to each other by different calls and pitches of voice.

In the pecking system of wild geese families, goose, gander, and goslings come first, followed by paired adults without young. Then come nonpaired adults, then unattached juveniles. The young in goose families which have some prestige, are better off and are more readily accepted than young geese in families with not so much clout.

In a fight, the goose that starts it is most often successful. There can be any number of fighters, but numbers do not necessarily mean victory. When there are many geese in one location, fights are apt to be more numerous.

Families respond to mutual defense. Geese with the largest number of goslings seem to be most favored in the order of combat.

When the family is about to fly, the signals are given by the gander. Sometimes, ganders appear to be the watchers for the family or the flock. Geese apparently don't post sentrys. In the molting period, geese are quiet. There is not so much fighting then. The molting period lasts about forty days.

Families tend to stay together in the goose world. But when the mother and father return north to nest, the young geese of the previous season are driven away.

Wild geese become mature in about two years and take mates then.

The Mississippi Flyway flock traditionally nests at James Bay, winters at Horseshoe Lake, near Cairo, Illinois, and at refuges adjoining, and naturally stops over at the Horicon Marsh in Wisconsin.

Yes, and to repeat, the Canada goose does mate for life; as long as one mate lives the other does not pair again.

However, if a mate dies or is lost, the other will take a new mate. Lovemaking among geese is preceded by display and movement of body and neck, and calls by the male. Wing flapping, diving, and frenzied dashing about are all part of goose lovemaking.

Young geese are promiscuous before they take mates, and are sometimes homosexual — males may attempt to make love to males.

On a day after a severe storm or blizzard in the spring, males fight other males viciously, and various forms of sexual activity seem to be speeded up.

Geese love to nest in elevated locations. They use the same nest sites more than one year. Geese are very faithful when nesting; they take excellent care of their eggs, protecting them in bad weather, shading them when the weather is too hot. When the goose leaves her nest, she covers it with light grass and small twigs. When she returns, she uncovers the eggs before settling down on them.

The molting period takes place in June and July. During this period, wild geese are flightless.

When intruders come near, the goose on the nest fluffs her feathers. When alarmed she raises her head, extending it upward. She seldom feeds during the incubation period. Her mate does feed. Perhaps he is building up his strength as a protector.

Usually, the goslings do not return to the nest after they once leave it.

The gander watches intently what goes on in his territory which is carefully defined. After the young leave the nest, the territory does not continue to exist. The pair occupying a territory protect it together against all comers. The gander will fight an intruding goose of either sex. When an intruder enters the territory calling, or honking, the protecting gander attacks savagely. If the intruder is silent, the attack is less violent.

Geese do a lot of bluffing, showing off. Fighting often does not take place when there is a lot of honking and muscular display. The gander always puts on a show of triumph when he routs an intruder. He honks, flaps his wings, and struts around, if on land. In the water, he rises, flapping and calling.

The family within the flock is not so easy to maintain. The little goslings, not long out of the eggs, and perhaps just in the water, cry when they are separated from their parents. The distress calls of the young are sharp peeping sounds, and as soon as the lost one is reunited with the family, the sharp peeps become softer, contented. The small goslings huddle around the mother and under her protecting body at times, always when it rains, and always at night. After the first week or so, the mother broods her flock less and less. The young are encouraged to become self-sufficient, strong.

If other geese come near while the family is young, the gander attacks savagely. The parents protecting the goslings do not usually honk; perhaps it is because honking attracts and causes attacks on the family from geese whose nests are near. And when goslings, which are not of the family, come near, they may be attacked by the parents and even by the small members of the family as well. The young ones nip at the visiting goslings and help to drive them away.

Sometimes, though, among the grasses of the nesting area, goslings who are lost find a home with strange parents. This doesn't happen when the wandering goslings are much more than a week old. When they are small, and about the same size as the goslings of the new family, they are sometimes adopted. When this occurs, the real parents of the adopted goslings have great trouble getting them to return. The new parents now defend the youngsters as their own.

The members of the flock have definite kinds of calls. A hissing sound is directed at other geese, or any intruder, who comes too near the nest. The hiss means that the goose or gander is very much alarmed. As the intruder comes closer, the hissing increases. When he goes away, the goose stops hissing and may begin to honk.

The gander's honk is loud and prolonged.

The goose gives short clipped honks. They both honk when they are warning intruders away from the nesting territory; when a mate moves away, the action brings honks from the other part of the pair who calls him or her to come back. Then, when the mates have been separated for a time and then come together, they greet each other with loud and prolonged honks. Human beings, watching geese from a distance, get to know the various tones of the greetings and the warnings. It almost becomes possible to interpret the honks as geese speech, and to fancy that they exchange actual conversation. In fact, some experts believe that there may be a greater sophistication in goose language then we realize; and that by various sounds, loudness, and pitch, the voices of the geese carry messages that have many varied meanings. The honks become very loud and long when an intruder approaches the flock, or approaches the family, or when a gosling gives his call of distress. When the flock is about to take flight, they honk, and often in flight, the honking continues. Possibly in flight, the geese call to one another; fear of separation may inspire the calls.

When the geese are near each other, they exchange a low, soft grunt. The grunting seems to be reserved for communication between the mates. It is used just before flight, when the gander, for instance, tries to induce his mate to take off with him. When the goose calls to the goslings, she uses about the same call: soft, urgent grunts, not so loud as the language used between the mates.

The gander has a special love call, too, that he uses when the pair have been newly mated. He uses it also when the pair have joined after a separation. Fondness, concern, is certainly expressed. The call is loud and sounds a bit like snoring. It is not at all like the distress call which both the gander and the goose may give when there is an attacker nearby.

The birds make poems possible.

Yet, there is little poetry in hunger.

Hunger which some do not rightly understand.

The search continues for goose and man.

When the flock is banded, or those parts of it which are captured for banding, the capture is often done by rocket nets. The nets are about sixty feet long by thirty feed wide. They are powered either by three or four steel rockets, almost like those shot on the Fourth of July. The rockets are attached to the nets — three along the back of the net, and the net is folded upon itself. Bait, corn usually, is placed on the ground in front of the net. When there is a sufficiently large number of the flock on the ground in front of the net, the rockets are fired. The net shoots out and settles over the feeding birds.

There is also a cannon net which works on the same principle as the rocket net. The difference is that instead of rockets, the cannon net uses mortar type shells, but the net settles over the birds in the same way. Once under the net, the birds are taken from it one at a time. The explosion of the net frightens the birds, of course. They thresh violently under the net, strive to fly, and sometimes injure themselves by the violence of their frenzy. Usually the birds become entangled rapidly. They quiet down when the scientist moves slowly, carefully. And a few of the birds, after they have been under the net for a half hour or so, may even begin to feed on the corn. The bird will likely struggle while the scientist is trying to get a firm hold, but once he has been fully captured he seems to know that he's conquered and stays very quiet through the banding process.

The flock is skilled at navigation, and apparently its navigational skill is the result of experience. A man uses all his senses in finding his way in the forest — his sight, his instinctive sense or awareness of direction, his knowledge of nature lore, his previous experience in the woods — all these things help man to find his way. In the flock, it is perhaps the same. Man is driven by a need to go somewhere and to arrive. Birds are impelled to go somewhere and to arrive. Why they go is because of their need: they must have food, they must survive weather which grows too severe, or they must find appropriate grounds for their nests. Their routes take them in directions which have been found excellent for them before; for them, or for their fathers, mothers, or many, many generations beyond. Knowledge of the way to go is passed from generation to generation through experience, through having been that way before, and because they have gone that way they have found food at the end of their journeys.

Why the flock originally, in a primeval world, chose the flyway from north to south, no man can say. But there are things that must have determined it: the knowledge in the flock that there must be water — so they followed the shorelines, and progressed from marsh to marsh; the force and direction of the wind — for during the months from September to November in Canada and in the north and central parts of the United States, the predominant flow of wind is from the northwest. The flock, no doubt, tended to drift downwind. There was also the far-reaching experience of the younger birds, who sometimes deviated from the main courses followed by their parents, to discover new feeding grounds, and new waters on which to alight and to rest.

The shorelines of the Great Lakes, the Mississippi River, were landmarks seen and followed. When the birds fly at seven, nine thousand feet, they don't need too many landmarks — a half dozen major topographical features may do. Just who it is that is sighting the features of the land, testing the wind currents, deciding when and where to stop, to rest, or to feed, nobody really knows. The bird out in front, the one at the head of the V — is certainly the leader; but whether he is the one who is doing the navigation — is another problem. Possibly the leader changes as the flight progresses. Many times the formation seems to change in character and shape, and birds change position.

The flock progresses by voice signals, doubtless, for in flight their voices are heard below. They apparently can hear each other for a long distance; and perhaps they do tell each other about the land, the water, the condition of their bodies, whether rest is necessary, or how far they are along the way to their goal. Migration flight is at a much higher altitude than flight to and from a feeding ground, and as the birds fly the route in migration, their contact with each other may be different than in short flight. Unless the flock is pressed by weather conditions or hunting pressure, they will sit out a bad wind, which retards their progress. And on the refuge, with migration time approaching, an approaching storm may well be a signal for the actual flight to begin.

Gray told Joe about the whole flyway concept. He hadn't known much about it in the early years of his labors at the marsh; but as the birds began to come more and more, he realized that there must be a pattern to their coming and going, and how they came. Nearly everybody who spoke of ducks and geese knew that there was a route they followed. Gray said that the routes were really identified by Frederic C. Lincoln, who called them the Atlantic, the Pacific, the Mississippi, and the Central flyways. The geese at Horicon Marsh, which traverse the country from the inland areas of the coasts of James Bay and the south coast of Hudson Bay, and thence come south after the nesting season, down the western side of Michigan and down the eastern sides of the states directly east of the Mississippi River, use the Mississippi Flyway. They stop over at Horicon Marsh and fly south in their migration to the refuges near Cairo, Illinois.

Somehow the ducks and geese know the route, though sometimes when one flyway merges near another, the birds might almost follow one or another by chance. When birds were removed from their original flyway, they were often discovered back in their original one. Some of the earliest experiments were conducted by Jack Miner. Miner located his sanctuary in Essex County, Ontario, and his was one of the earliest bird sanctuaries established in North America. Jack Miner built his first pond and set out decoys to attract geese in 1904, but wasn't able to lure a goose family until 1908. Slowly the geese built up in numbers, but they used the refuge only in the spring. After 1915, though, the birds used it in the fall also.

The original Miner grounds included about seventeen acres; and then other land purchases expanded the sanctuary, and corn, rye, and timothy were planted. The birds came, stayed until November or December, and indeed, some stayed all winter. Miner banded many birds and was a pioneer in discovering the habits of the flock.

The flock, in its willing adaptation to conditions established by man, has caused problems. The geese have radically changed their former habits of flying the entire length of the flyway, from the nesting grounds to the Gulf Coast. Now they "short-stop" at the refuges along the way, and often they never go any further than Horseshoe Lake in southern Illinois. The winter is not severe there; and in any case, as long as a bird has food and water,

he doesn't greatly care about temperature. He will certainly survive.

The "short-stopping" developed in the following way: the flock, nesting in Canada, once flew southward through the United States. All along the route they were harassed by hunters whose endless shooting kept the flock moving and decreased their numbers.

As the situation became critical, and the population of the flock decreased and decreased, a series of refuges were developed along the migration route. Land was purchased, management systems set up, and food was planted. The geese, little by little, responded. They found it most pleasant to stop at a well-provisioned refuge where they were protected; and they soon learned where the refuges were located and became sensitive to the exact boundaries where the protection ceased.

Hunters too responded to the refuge idea, for the concentrations of geese made hunting easier, and it was no trouble at all to take a goose or so in the areas around the refuges.

At first, after the refuges were established, the geese simply remained for awhile, then they completed their journey to the south. As time went on, however, and the food increased at the refuges, many of the birds stopped going further south entirely. Several generations which did not go on changed the flock's habits completely. And the hunting pressure on the fewer geese who did finish their migration caused them further to abandon the trip. Among hunters further south, the distress was acute. Large investments had been made in hunting lodges, in restaurants, and motels, all geared to serve the goose hunter. When there were no geese, the situation became unbearable. The southern hunters complained about the northern refuges, and in some cases, attempts were made to distribute the flock, to send it on south. But this failed. The geese liked the refuge idea and refused to move on.

Sometimes the natives back in the country complained.

"Them geese belongs to us folks hereabouts," Jack Maxwell told Joe. "Them geese is part of our traditions. We folks have always lived around here. Them birds have been comin' forever. They come and land around here and we hunts 'em. Lordy, the fun we had. You take the geese away from us, there is going to be trouble.

"Why, I recall my daddy goin' out to the river and comin' back sometimes with twenty, thirty geese. He was one hell of a shot, daddy was. He had him an old ten gauge he calls Betsy, or Susabel. Had a barrel about forty inches long. Called her his goose gun.

"Shucks, he could down a goose near as far as he could see him. That's what daddy says. Don't hold with them guys that tries to get the birds away from us river folks. No sense to that. There is plenty of geese. Too many. Hell, they will eat up all the crops; you don't go out and shoot 'em.

"Don't hold with puttin' all that feed for the birds to draw 'em away. Ain't like it used to be. Geese goes up to the refuge and eats and stays around there. You can pick off a goose now and then maybe, but it ain't like it used to be. And how about them folks in Louisiana that used to have the geese come every winter. How about them folks?

"There ain't hardly a goose goes down there anymore. The refuges up north has them all cornered. Them guys down south are starving for birds.

"Heard tell them was a lot of lawsuits against them state men that have got the geese stoppin' up north. I would sure be asuin' them people, too. Had me a huntin' club and nobody come, because there wasn't no birds, and them guys up north killin' as many as they want.

"Hell, we folks know what's goin' on. Them state guys settin' out there potting as many geese as they want. Us natives starving. Well, I tell you what. I am going to kill me a goose whenever I feel like doin' it. Anytime. You get that? I ain't no different than my daddy was. That's what he done. Anytime. Just take old Betsy and kill him a goose.

"This conservation stuff. That is crap. You know it is crap. Why, they got to let things alone. Us folks will take care of all the goose protection they need. We ain't gonna kill them all, you know that. Them state guys is doing too much. All them birds will die anyhow.

"Why, I seen plenty of times how them young guys come from the university to put bands on them birds. What do they do that

for? If they would mark just the biggest geese so's us folks would know which was the best, that would be all right. But that ain't the reason. Ain't no way tellin' what them guys got in mind.

"Ought to let things alone. Just the way they used to be. Daddy and grandpa was around, they wouldn't stand for it like it is. Rich people come and kill all the geese. Us poor folks don't have a good chance to get geese. Can't afford it. Them rich guys from Chicago come every week. Kill, kill, kill, that's what they do. Us guys got nothin'.

Debts, that's what we got."

Until 1936, the Mississippi Flyway had never had a goose census taken. Millions of birds had passed over the route through the centuries. Man had no idea how many there were. There were indications of course. In 1895, two partners in the market-hunting business killed 2,280 geese — more than 50 a day. There were wild geese hanging in front of every market in Cairo, and every restaurant in 1885 had wild goose on its menu. There was no refrigeration anywhere in those days and, to dispose of the birds, dealers were selling them for as little as thirty or forty cents a bird.

In 1936, they counted the geese; they took them by blocks in certain river areas and did the best they could. They counted 47,510. The count was probably not very accurate, for there were many more geese than that number in the region. But it gave the conservation men a beginning. In 1940, it became very apparent, through other area censuses, that the Mississippi River Flyway flock of Canada geese was decreasing. The floods that had kept the sandbars clean and had nourished the shoots of willow upon which the geese like to browse had been at least partly controlled. Also the farmers in the area were changing from large acreages of corn to soybeans as a major crop. The geese did not like to feed on soybeans as much as upon corn, and indeed, the beans often led to "bound crops," wherein the geese died from the swelling of the beans. And the hunters were taking more and more birds. The government had also created the channel system of the Mississippi River, and the growing numbers of large barge tows and hooting tugs kept the waters in turmoil, and made the birds nervous.

There is always winter, a time to fly away.

But there are wounded ones who cannot fly and walk sadly.

They fumble among long-picked corn.

They must sense the old bald eagle, just a blur, who preys upon them.

They wait everything out.

The brook silently speaks the tragedy.

When Joe drifted the flatboat up to the dock at his place, he could predict about what his day would be. Mary would have the breakfast ready; and when he came in from fishing, he was always very hungry. She'd have made hot cereal, and maybe a pan of hot baking powder biscuits, fried eggs, of course, and some homemade pork sausage. Oh yes, and milk gravy. She made that very, very well. Joe had been raised on milk gravy and hot biscuits. It was a comforting thought to know that the first part of his day would go well at Mary's table. His life wouldn't have been much, he guessed, without the familiar things that Mary did to please him and to keep him contented. He realized that he was restless, and that it must worry Mary. She was content enough in her home, doing what she liked to do, working with her hands, visiting, doing her church work, and reading. But himself — well, his day would be about the same as yesterday.

After breakfast he'd probably do a few odd jobs around the place: there was a board in the porch floor that had to be replaced, and after he'd fixed that he would maybe take the car and go over to Beaver Dam to visit awhile with Bill Field. Bill had worked on the marsh about as long as Joe had. Bill retired last year, and they gave him a big retirement party, same as they had Joe. It was nice, of course, that they did that, but Joe doubted that what retiring from a place like the Horicon Marsh meant to him, or to Bill, could ever be the same to a governmental agency. Old-timers really wanted to keep on being needed and to have their years of experience and knowledge put to some really good use. But that wasn't the way it worked. Anyway, he and Bill had

their great memories. As Joe went to the tank in a corner of his backyard where he kept live fish, he thought about some of the things he and Bill had done together. Bill had come to work at the marsh about 1936, not too long after Joe had started. Bill's first assignment had been at Iron River. Fred Miner had been warden up there then, and Bill had worked with him and learned about doing warden's work. Then they assigned Bill to Vernon County. Joe thought it was in April 1936 that Bill was told he was going to be sent east to Beaver Dam. Joe was reminded of the way he and Mary had finally got together; for Bill called up the girl he was engaged to in Viroqua and said to her that he was going to Beaver Dam and wished they could get married. Three days later they were married, and with about fifty dollars in Bill's pocket, they moved. The young couples, the Malones and Fields, had been well acquainted in those early years. Bill stayed as warden until 1947, when he was put in charge of the commercial licenses in Wisconsin. Bill could see then, and he and Joe often talked of it, that the marshes, the wetlands, were disappearing fast. Bill established more licensed muskrat farms than anytime in Wisconsin's history. The reason was, a farmer looked over his back forty, and he was either going to plow it, or drain it, or do something useful with it. Wisconsin farmers, Bill knew, were restless. They had to be, or they wouldn't be farming very long. Bill convinced a lot of farmers that having a muskrat farm with a real low state fee and no license was a good business investment. The animals, under Wisconsin law, became personal property when a game farm was established. A person could start a muskrat farm, a bird farm, a deer farm, beaver, skunk, almost any kind of a wildlife farm was possible.

The side benefits, as Bill and Joe had seen them, were remarkable. A farmer, keeping his marsh for the muskrats, had many, many side benefits, and they were benefits for the general public as well. The state would dredge a marsh with ditches twelve feet across and five feet deep, for two dollars a rod. And many good things transpired. The rats didn't freeze out of their houses any longer — when the water froze clear to the bottom, and the rat couldn't get back home. The ditches became breeding grounds for minnows, and nesting sites for birds. Joe had tried such a farm himself.

As an observation on the disappearance of the wetlands, Joe thought that one of the saddest possible sights was a pair of Canada geese he had once seen standing in an earth-covered area that had once been a small marsh. The pair had stopped at this place every spring on their northward migration, for there was food to be had there. The small marsh was resting place for a few birds. Then one day the heavy machines came. A highway was being constructed a short distance away. Excavated earth was pushed into the marsh. It was said by the highway workers that this would be a good thing. The marshland was of no value, and it made a perfect dumpground for unneeded earth.

But the geese did not understand what the men were doing. They stood confused and lonely on the piles of earth and uttered low sad sounds. They walked around on the top of the piles, seeking with their bills for the grasses and roots they had once found in the marsh waters. There would never be a marsh in that place again.

The two geese lingered most of an entire day.

But the children and grandchildren of the future probably would never see wild ducks and geese in their area, stopping to feed, or to nest. Little by little, except for the refuges, the birds were being displaced and forced to congregate on the refuges, and to seek, as they have done, nesting sites in the far north.

But the sites in the far north are being threatened, too.

The James Bay region, where the Canada geese nest, is being threatened by great power dams.

If the passenger pigeon is extinct, the Canada goose is certainly not extinct. In places its numbers increase. Yet in some locations in America, the Canada goose is also dead. Old books tell how there were once innumerable geese nesting in Indiana and Iowa. Minnesota had its thousands and thousands of nesting Canadas. In Manitoba and in the whole upper third of the Mississippi Valley, even as far down as Saint Louis, and, some say, even as far south as western Mississippi, there were nesting birds. Now no geese breed in these locations.

And it is not entirely because the marshes and potholes have been drained. Partly it is because the geese with the memory of nesting in the southern places are gone. There are no birds now to carry forward the older traditions.

And so the old nesting grounds lie silent. There are no sounds of nesting geese, and little by little, the waters drain from the marshes.

Drainage of marshy places has been going on for many years. The development of heavy machines, capable of moving as much earth in an hour as a hundred teams of mules and two hundred men could move in a day, has quickened the disappearance of the small marshes. Federal funds have been available to hurry the death of the small marsh, and nobody has much cared, except the lonely birds when they attempt to return, and a small organization or two.

Most of the large marshes disappeared long ago. As early as 1909, plans were made to drain the great Horicon Marsh basin and to turn it to agriculture. That effort failed; but in many other places it has not failed.

The people have been told that upland waters must be retained to protect lands from flood and drought; great dam projects are undertaken, and the wildlife disappears, or becomes a stepchild of a drainage project — the argument for water conservation carries little weight with the ditching and draining agencies, or with the highway builders.

When the small marshes lose their water, the waterfowl breeding traditions are also lost.

The Canada goose has not returned to the prairie nesting sites for a long, long while. But the ducks have fought longer. Now the ducks have almost lost the fight.

The urge has been for land and more land for farming, to get rid of the water, to provide land for an ever increasing human population. The arguments have painted the future as both bright and demanding; children and grandchildren will have great need of the land that the waters once covered.

A great buck watches death.

The hunter fires upward. The good hunters kill;
the bad hunters maim.

The fullness of life and the possibility of death are everywhere.

Joe put the morning bullheads he had caught and had kept alive into the tank. He kept fresh water running into the tank all the time, and the fish could stay in it indefinitely. Mary liked to take them directly from the fresh water.

He stood in the yard for a moment, yawned, feeling a little sleepy, but keeping an ear open for sounds of geese in the high sky. They would be going out to feed about now. There would be freezes soon, and ice coming on the ditches and the wide, shallow places in the river. He and Bill Yeats had seen some geese get frozen in one time. It was the only time that Joe had ever seen a thing like that happen, and he guessed it wouldn't have happened, except that freeze came unbelievably fast. There was a thin ice, and some water on top of it, when the storm swirled down — Joe thought it was in 1940, Armistice Day, in November, anyway, and he remembered that a lot of hunters had actually died that day — none on the Horicon Marsh; but on the Mississippi River, a lot of them died when they were marooned without proper supplies and clothing. One hunter that Joe knew had saved himself by putting live decoys inside his hunting coat. The ducks kept him warm enough to survive.

That morning, early, after the storm, he and Bill had been out, and they heard the weak honks from the shallow place. They found geese on the ice. Several of the birds were dead, but a number were still alive, and one old gander honked defiantly as they came to him, walking gingerly on the ice. They were able to free fifteen or twenty birds. Some of them moved slowly, or hardly at all. But the old gander took right off, circled once over the place, and departed.

The incident became a sort of personal legend with Joe and Bill, for geese weren't much seen around the marsh then. The flock had probably become lost in the storm and had come down when there was still enough light to reflect on the ice which, they supposed, the birds had mistaken for open water.

The way he and Bill felt about things was the same way that nearly all the old-timers on the marsh felt. They knew that the groups at the marsh now seemed to be divided. There were the young men who were currently doing the management. And there was the retired group of state men and the local old-timers who had always lived and hunted on the marsh. These guys who were once the marsh "outlaws," breaking a game law occasionally, but master conservationists in their own way, and the old state men, were now together in a closeness they had never known when they were younger. The older men wished they could still participate with the younger, active men, but they couldn't, really.

The way the old ones felt, it was as though hunting and fishing and game management had a mastery, a true devotion attached to it. Regard for wildlife had a mystic quality that came from many, many years of love, of devoted service, of sport.

There were arrows of red in the sky, and the wind across the marsh was coming in puffs that opened the tall brown cattails and marsh grass. In and among the stems and fronds, the wind wove mats and patterns. Joe glanced at the sky, always anticipating the lines of wild geese. Now there were none. They had gone already into the fields for corn. But he could go nowhere save into his own past, seeking how the wild birds caused the demarcations of his life. To do so, he must seek eternally into the past, and it was as though he must bring the cloying nostalgia into his present in order to breathe, to exist, so much was he attached to what had happened, had gone before. And suddenly Joe wondered whether this was really the way he should go. It was self-pity he felt, and if he were being self-pitying, wasn't that a sign of his self-defeat; for if the past to him was only beautiful and the present full of pessimism and doubt, then what hope was there of something beyond pessimism?

The wild geese, perhaps all nature, set their own way and their own tempo. Left alone, the birds, the animals, the wetlands, the hills, the valleys, and all growing things would repeat their own cycles, and they would survive until the time of their cycles ran out. But the problem of the wild things, all wild creatures, was man. They must exist in a world in which man shaped their environments to his ends. It didn't matter really that the ends which man foresaw were sometimes envisioned in the hope of aiding nature; this signified nothing, for the ends were created by man in a world in which there were too many men.

How, indeed, could there be an attitude that was not pessimistic, when there was such rush to use the land and the waters, to build great hydroelectric power plants in the far north, at James Bay, for example, which would destroy nesting places of the Mississippi Flyway flock of the Canada geese?

Joe knew that the eelgrass of the taiga would disappear from the feeding areas there; that the otters, bears, caribou, mink, rabbits, and porcupines would be forced from the great subartic forests as the water gathered. He knew that over 135,000 square miles which the Cree Indians had hunted for hundreds of years, their hunting grounds, would disappear.

The taiga was a long, long way from the Horicon Marsh; but the taiga was a part of the whole plan by which both the wild geese and Joe Malone regulated the meaning of their lives.

How other than with pessimism could he view the entire future?

He heard Mary in the kitchen, and he thought again of her simple faith in God. She easily accepted the eternal and omnipotent wisdom in governance which had nothing to do with the pursuits of man. Mary was happy in her acceptance of an overriding, good God, and she herself did not expect much more than good for her children and for him, Joe.

Did he, Joe Malone, expect too much?

Did he really want the voice of God to articulate itself from every bush that might also burn?

Joe didn't want or expect that. He was only certain that he could never personally understand what would be the direction of man in his love for, and in his destruction of, the beauty and loneliness of nature.

The wind wove the reeds, and a soft sound, a humming, far and mysterious, seemed to emanate from the middle of the marsh beyond Joe's house. It might have been a sound of wind in trees, or over far wires; or it may have been an echo of traffic from some distant highway. Wind and sound and the perplexity of not knowing where he was seemed to be Joe's present awareness. The past, as he thought of it, and as he heard Mary begin to sing in the kitchen, had little point suddenly.

Joe looked upward, hearing the voices of geese above him. The line they made in the sky was ragged, straggling. Suddenly it began to reform and became a clear, firm V.

"What am I wondering about myself for," Joe said aloud; and a meaning, out of the turmoil he had been in since his retirement, became clear to him as he watched the birds. He wasn't through because he was old, or tired. He wasn't through because he wasn't working at the marsh any longer. He wasn't through anymore than any moment in the time span of any generation of Canada geese was ended. Nothing ended. Moment by moment simply merged into moments. The perception of man was immediate and was perforce of now.

"And that is where I have been in error," Joe said. "The past became an end in itself. But to the geese, the past is something they have learned. The past is not their necessity; there is to them only the immediacy of corn, flight, migration, reproduction, of death from the hunter's gun or the eagle's talons.

"And I, the man, have hoped to see clear through to the end. I can't. I guide my life from the past, just as the wild geese learn the routes of their migrations. But they do not see to the ends of their lives. I cannot see to the end of mine, nor to the end of the marsh, nor to the end of migration. Man is not God."

Joe looked again at the disappearing line of the geese, and the flash of beauty he saw in their way of going was enough. He brightened, wondered why he had been so depressed, and he moved cheerfully into Mary's small world of snatches of hymns, of hot biscuits, gravy, and love for him. He had, after all, lived it all. He had known the hazards of birds and of men. It was enough. He believed he could accept the past for what it was, and the future for what it might offer of hope.

But the thing that cheered him was a realization of his true confidence in himself, because of what he had been and of what he was now. In the mysterious and miraculous way that knowledge sometimes comes, he knew his ability to appreciate and to accept.

He sat down at the red checked cloth-covered table and waited with pleasure for Mary to say her table grace. She had done that all their lives together.

Life abundant in all seasons. It is the meaning of my search, to love, to preserve . . .

to watch and guard the young things . . .

to see the butterflies in summer . . .

to realize the aching to give and to receive . . .

to know the beauty of the bird in flight . . .

to appreciate total beauty . . .

to understand the complexity of life.

I know man's tracks fall away.

Yet, I can dream about the wetlands, the life upon them, and I can hope. I am here for a day, but my actions have meaning.

At the end, the birds remain and they climb to the sky as they have for thousands of years.